TEDDY BEARS ON A TANDEM

Best wishes
from Ingrid, Sean
and Kate
x

TEDDY BEARS ON A TANDEM

Kate Tomlinson aged 15
and Kate's Mum aged 48

Matador
9 Priory Business Park,
Wistow Road, Kibworth Beauchamp,
Leicestershire. LE8 0RX
Tel: 0116 279 2299
Email: books@troubador.co.uk
Web: www.troubador.co.uk/matador
Twitter: @matadorbooks

ISBN 978 1788036 238

British Library Cataloguing in Publication Data.
A catalogue record for this book is available from the British Library.

Printed and bound by CPI Group (UK) Ltd, Croydon, CR0 4YY
Typeset in 12pt Sabon MT by Troubador Publishing Ltd, Leicester, UK

Matador is an imprint of Troubador Publishing Ltd

In Memory of Tom, my Grandad, who always enthusiastically supported us, and often accompanied us on our adventures.

'Looking back I don't think I fully understood the concept of leaving home to travel the world for two years. The reality of it only really dawned on me after the first year. I didn't question the fact that my parents, who had no previous experience of cycle touring, had planned their journey using an atlas that was twenty years out of date. At that age I just accepted whatever my parents planned for me.

I mean grown ups are sensible and always know what they are doing, right?'

"I first met Ingrid Sean and Kate or 'Baby Kate' as she is still actually known, back in 2008. Since that first meeting I've had the pleasure of hearing many a tale of both their amazing world wide adventures as a family, from cycling through North and South America, to 'keeping it local' with kayaking trips around the Isle of Skye. Ingrid's instinctive eye for photography has also captured some exceptional moments from their trips, which brings to life these frankly exhausting escapades- "you did what?!" "Yup, look! Here's a picture!"...

To think they've travelled the world as a family, often in a mode of transport that not many families would take on; Tandem anyone? Kayak family trip? is testament to their spirit of adventure, their lust for life but also a strong indication, that they're beautifully nuts. Or just very keen to avoid arguments about which music gets played in the car. To be honest, I'm just surprised it's taken them this long to produce their first book....but then the pages have probably just dried out from all that kayaking with whales..."

Comedian Greg McHugh (aka Gary Tank Commander)

Contents

INTRODUCTION

Smells like Trip!

I can always tell when an adventure is about to happen in our household. The place has a distinctive smell about it.

It's a combination of the fusty scent of inside of tent and the rubbery odour of well used wetsuits. Add to that a subtle dash of methylated spirits and a hint of mildew from worn out holdalls and there it is – the smell of Trip! It's a smell that I have been familiar with for as long as I can remember.

One day, when I was eight years old, I arrived home from school and there was a definite whiff of 'Trip' in the air. The contents of our outdoor equipment store, aka the cupboard under the stairs, were piled up in the hallway. Maps were spread out across the kitchen floor and the cats were looking out of sorts.

'Here we go' I muttered to myself. 'Mum's been looking at the atlas again!'

'Hey Kate!' said Dad, peering out from behind a pile of travel guides. 'How would you feel about missing school for two years and going on a 16,000 mile bike journey?'

'Can Kaya and Élan come too?' I asked, referring to my best friends.

'I don't think their parents would let them' replied Mum. 'Their families would miss them too much if they were away on the other side of the world for such a long time.'

I thought for a minute.

'Can I have a new Bratz doll then?' I asked.

In those days I was relatively easy to bribe. The occasional new toy or ice cream was generally enough to keep me happy throughout our long adventures in distant places. Nowadays I drive a harder bargain. Before I agree to spend the whole of next summer squashed up in a tiny tent between two smelly argumentative parents, they'll have to promise me a weekend festival ticket to T in the Park at LEAST!

I am 15 years old and my parents have yet to take me on holiday!

By holiday I mean one of those events where I'd be allowed to stay in a nice hotel with a balcony and a swimming pool, as opposed to a tent pitched on a cliff top next to a lagoon full of icebergs.

I wouldn't be expected to share the washing facilities with giant cockroaches or the bed with a trail of ants.

I would eat my meals at a table, not huddled around a camping stove on the beach in the rain and it wouldn't be necessary to hang our food in a tree each night to prevent the bears from eating it (or us).

On one of these imaginary vacations, we wouldn't wear the same set of clothes for months at a time and we'd come home with all over suntans instead of brown hands, burnt faces and bodies which look as if they have never been exposed to daylight.

During this fortnight of decadent luxury Dad wouldn't wake up in a panic in the middle of the night worrying that somebody might be about to drive over (or eat) the tent.

Mum doesn't have a mystery to solve

Enid Blyton has a lot to answer for. As a child my Mum was completely hooked on her books, especially the stories about the 'Famous Five', a group of children and their dog, Timmy who lived in Cornwall and had amazingly exciting adventures every single holiday. Mum longed for her life to be like theirs. She modelled herself on her favourite 'Famous Five' character, George, a tomboy whose real name was Georgina, and for two years she insisted that everyone including her friends, parents and teachers call her George as well.

When she wasn't being chased by angry land owners for trespassing in derelict buildings or disused quarries, she was busy spying on her neighbours in the hope of discovering suspicious activities, and compiling long lists of clues and plans, written in code or with invisible ink made from lemon juice. She carried a torch and a skipping rope in her pocket at all times in preparation for the time when she, like George, would be kidnapped by villains in the dead of night and could escape from the window of a hidden tower.

By the time she was a teenager Mum had started to become disillusioned with the lack of secret passageways, smugglers caves and mysterious ruined castles in her own life. Despite years of tapping walls and sticking her head up chimneys, she hadn't discovered any trap doors or rooms concealed behind wooden panels. Nor had she found a single map indicating the location of an underground tunnel leading beneath the sea to a forbidden island heaving with dungeons and treasure.

Although she had scanned the night skies religiously for years, there was a disheartening absence of flashing lights on the horizon relaying coded messages from one criminal to another. Disappointingly the neighbours that she spied on turned out to be boring law abiding citizens and inexplicably nobody seemed to be the least bit interested in kidnapping her.

In retrospect she has decided that this could have had something to do with the fact that her Dad was only a French teacher, unlike George's father, Uncle Quentin, who was a famous scientist experimenting with secret formulae, and that a briefcase full of worksheets displaying the verb 'to be' in all its different tenses probably didn't present the same allure to thugs and villains as government sensitive documents.

Eventually, after realising that Enid Blyton had filled her head with false expectations of what was likely to happen during the average school holiday, Mum turned to outdoor pursuits instead. She joined the 4As Adventure Club in Ambleside and when she left school she went to teacher training college there to study Outdoor Education;

Which is where she met my Dad who was working in a climbing café, having recently finished a fine arts degree at University (or playschool as Grandad called it) He was the vegetarian chef and Mum used to go in every day for a bacon sandwich while she was writing her dissertation.

He had long hair, a woolly rainbow jumper and baggy patchwork trousers. He used to drive around in a bright green and red Citroen Dianne with the roof rolled down and his Springer spaniel, Bilbo sitting in the passenger seat, his long brown ears flying back in the wind as reggae music blared out of the car stereo. (Bilbo's ears that is, not Dad's).

He tricked my Mum into going on a date with her by pretending that he had never been climbing before and wanted somebody to take him out. Then he lured her in to his house with the chat up line of 'Would you like to come in and see my sculptures?'

The two of them bought a big old hippy bus together, filled it with patchworks, candles, incense and weavings, and spent the next decade climbing, kayaking and breaking down in obscure and inconvenient places.

They travelled around between farms and tree nurseries, finding seasonal work to fund their summer kayaking expeditions which were mainly in Alaska.

Then after ten years I arrived on the scene!

An Unexpected Adventure

My parents were not expecting to have children so it came as quite a surprise when I appeared in their lives. In fact, for the first four months of my existence, my own mother mistook me for a beer belly.

They both agree that having me was the biggest, scariest but also the best adventure of their lives. They were finally about to become responsible adults.

They moved out of their big red bus and parked it next to their new, grown up house in Achmore in the Scottish Highlands. The bus is now used as a workshop for Dad to make his clay sculptures in.

Achmore is a lovely place to live and Mum and Dad were quite happy with their new life but they did wonder if being parents would mean no more going off on big adventures. They thought that the adventures which they had been planning would probably have to be put off for the next few years.

However I had other ideas! Some people believe that children choose their parents. If that's the case then I must said 'Please can mine be bonkers!' According to them, when I was a baby, I had to be on the move all the time.

They think it might be because I was conceived in a travelling bus (yeuch!) or because they were driving round Scotland Munro bagging as I was developing from beer belly to full term baby, but I was only content if I was being walked in the baby carrier, pushed in the pram or driven in the car. The moment Mum tried to put me down I would sense that the motion had ceased and I'd start screaming. For two years I wouldn't allow my parents to sit down to read a book, watch TV or to eat a meal with both hands.

After six months Mum decided that if she was going to spend the foreseeable future slogging up and down hills all day with me on her back then she might as well go and do it somewhere different and exotic so they booked flights to Kathmandu and when I was ten months old we all went trekking in the Annapurna region of the Nepal Himalayas.

CHAPTER 1

TREKKING IN THE HIMALAYAS

Nappies and Nits in Nepal

My very first toddler steps were taken at an altitude of 3300 metres in the rooftop room of a tea house at the village of Pisang in the foothills of Annapurna.

We arrived at the village of Besi Sahar at the beginning of the Annapurna Circuit in late September after a nine hour ride on a stiflingly hot and overcrowded local bus. Mum remembers this journey as the most gruelling part of the trek. For a while the aisle was so crammed she had to have a complete stranger sitting on her knee, as well as me latched onto a nipple.

Some people brought chickens and even the occasional goat on board with them. Another fifteen passengers clung to the roof outside as the bus was driven along narrow, busy roads, weaving through fresh landslides and barely slowing down for oncoming traffic as it skirted the edge of precipitous cliffs with barely an inch to spare. The sight of wrecked upside down buses in the river gorges hundreds of feet below didn't exactly inspire my parents with confidence.

They were glad to have the company of their friends, Ian and Jane and their three year old son Freddy who trekked with us for the first three weeks along with our guide, Tendu Sherpa. Our porter, Karma carried all my nappies and baby meals, Mum carried our clothes and sleeping bags and Dad carried me.

Mum had brought packets of dried baby meals for me to eat but once I'd tried the meals which were served at the tea houses I lost interest in my baby food and Mum gave it away. Pancakes, omelettes and fried potatoes were much tastier and I loved dal baht, a meal of lentils, rice and curried vegetables eaten by the Nepalese twice a day, although Mum continued to act as the drinks machine for another two years.

I had my baths in the big metal pans that are used for cooking and washing. We couldn't bring many toys so Mum and Dad improvised by fetching big pots and wooden spoons from the kitchen or big bunches of keys for me to play with.

The Annapurna Circuit is very popular so the people there, who are used to seeing crowds of tourists, don't usually pay much attention to passing foreigners but hardly anybody there had seen a white baby in real life before. With my blonde ringlets, blue eyes and rosy cheeks I attracted a lot of attention. Mum said she felt like the Pied Piper sometimes because there was always a trail of children following her. Everywhere we went women wanted to hold me and take me into their houses to show their families.

I can't remember anything about my first trip to Nepal. Mum says that's not surprising considering that I was asleep for most of the day while they toiled up the steep steps of the foothills with me in my carrier. It was only when we got into the tea houses and all the other people were relaxing, that I woke up ready to party. I was crawling at top speed by now and they had to keep an eye on me as there were rickety stairs, dirty floorboards with rusty nails and steep drops everywhere which I was eager to explore.

The rooms were separated from one another by thin sheets of wood meaning that any sounds that were made could be easily heard by all the other trekkers. Poor Mum ended up having to feed me most of the night so I didn't cry and disturb everyone. Mum says this was quite tiring for her, especially when she was huddled under a blanket at the higher altitudes where the dark unlit rooms dropped to well below freezing during the night.

At the lower altitudes there were gigantic spiders crawling up the walls of the tea houses, as well as leeches clinging to everyone's ankles. To be honest I'm more than happy to have no recollection of that!

One night when we were staying at Manang I was so fractious that Mum and Dad were worried about me. They had taken very strict precautions to avoid altitude sickness but, because babies can't talk and they cry for many different reasons, it was difficult to tell exactly what was troubling me. To be on the safe side they woke Karma up and they carried me down hill to the last village at 2 o clock in the morning, hoping that the 100 metre decrease in altitude would help. We couldn't find a tea house open at that time so we ended up sleeping on cushions in a barn.

Next day they took me to see a doctor who didn't think that there was anything seriously wrong with me so we returned to Manang. A few hours later however our heads started to itch like mad. On closer inspection it turned out that our hair was crawling with big black lice. Karma found this hilarious and insisted upon going through our hair every night with a nit comb until there was a pile of wriggling creepy crawlies on the table.

He never managed to get rid of them all though and they came back to Scotland with us where it took a bottle of tea tree oil and two doses of anti louse lotion to finally kill the whole lot. Mum was even considering getting all of our heads shaved. She reckons that being hatched at altitude must have

made them into indestructible super nits with extra powerful hearts and lungs.

Because of my age, my parents decided that it would probably be unwise to carry me over the 5416 metre Thorang La Pass so they trekked both sides of the circuit instead meaning that we were all well acclimatised for our trek to Annapurna Base Camp at 4130 metres in the middle of November.

When we arrived at the top, the innkeeper from the tea house where we spent the night told Mum and Dad that I was the youngest person they had ever seen up there.

Bubble Baths on the Base Camp Trek
Toddler Tantrums at Tengboche

The next year we all went to the Khumbu region of Nepal. My Grandad, Tom came with us this time so there were three generations of trekking Tomlinsons together.

I was eighteen months old so I was able to walk short stretches but only if two people stood on either side of me, holding my hands and shouting 'one, two, three whee!' while they lifted me up the steps. The paths in the Himalayas are nearly all steps.

I was just beginning to talk and some of my first words were yak, bridge and flag. One of my very first real memories that didn't come from looking at photographs is of turning a big Buddhist prayer wheel. When you pass a religious monument in Nepal, such as a chorten, gompa or mani wall, you are supposed to walk to the left of them or go around them in a clockwise fashion. To this day I still have a habit of walking around obstacles in this way.

This trek took us right past Karma's farmhouse so Mum had saved up some of my old baby clothes to present to his year old son. We were invited inside to meet the family who

gave us cups of warm milk, fresh from the yak that lived downstairs.

This year I was much more interested in my surroundings, especially baby goats and kittens and I enjoyed meeting other children of my age. I still kept my parents awake half the night though and sometimes got them into trouble with other trekkers. One day I was having great fun playing with the bubbles in my big metal pan bathtub when there was an angry knock on the door. I had splashed around so much that the water had spilled out and seeped through the cracks in the floorboards and onto the heads of the trekkers in the room below while they were sleeping!

A daily bath was necessary as my new favourite hobby was grubbing around in the dirt. The ground, thick with dust, dung and bits of rubbish was altogether more interesting than a sandpit. Consequently my hands, my face and my clothes were constantly filthy. Mum believes that this early exposure to germs has helped to build up my immune system which is why I don't get ill very often. In other words her lack of attention to hygiene is a parenting quality of which she can be proud. Thank goodness I wasn't one of those toddlers who put everything that they find on the ground straight into their mouths.

I had started to have tantrums at this age which occasionally attracted disapproving glances and comments from other trekkers who were trying to write up their journals or read in peace. The most spectacular of these was when a well meaning tourist gave me three chewy toffees one night. It was the first time I had tasted sweets and I was all smiles until I had finished the last one. When Mum refused to give me any more the whole lodge was subjected to my ear splitting shrieks of 'TWEEEEEEETIES!' until Grandad put me in the carrier and took me for a walk around the village.

The tables were turned in 2013 when I was twelve and we all returned to Nepal to hike to Kala Patthar above Everest

Base Camp. This time I was the one having to listen to them whingeing and grumbling as they struggled to keep up with me.

My favourite memory of this trip was at Gorak Shep, the highest village before Everest Base Camp. It was October 31st and I was feeling a little bit sad to be missing Halloween at home because it is my favourite night of the year. To cheer me up Mum made up a treasure hunt for me with a trail of silly, spooky picture clues leading to a frozen pile of stones where Dad had hidden a Mars Bar and a Bounty.

At this altitude chocolate bars like this cost as much as £2 each because everything has to be carried in on the backs of porters. Also our budget was running low so, although it was nothing like the size of my usual trick or treat stash, it was extra special. I felt like Charlie in Charlie and the Chocolate factory when he ate his annual birthday chocolate bar, savouring every tiny little piece!

CHAPTER TWO

ADVENTURES IN A KAYAK

Polished Pink Nails for Watching the Whales

As a child the thing that Mum longed for more than anything in the world was to own a little boat so that she, like George, could row out to explore remote islands where sinister things would undoubtedly be going on. Unfortunately her parents, who couldn't swim, were afraid that she might drown so she was never allowed to have one.

Once she tried to build a raft of her own from branches, skipping rope and string. It took her 3 weeks to construct and all of ten seconds for the 'Ship of Adventure' to fall apart and sink to the bottom of the Coniston Water while the grown ups fell about laughing and she had a tantrum.

Dad, on the other hand, was put in a kayak and sent off down grade 3 river rapids in January from such a young age that he was barely tall enough to see out of the top of his buoyancy aid.

For one of these reasons my parents thought it would be a good idea for me to spend half my childhood floating around at sea in a small boat. As soon as I was old enough to sit still by myself they bought a folding kayak especially designed for three people with a cockpit and seat for a child in the middle.

They tried it out first in the sea lochs near our home and paddling around the Greek Island of Milos and found that, like when I was in the backpack, the movement of the water usually lulled me to sleep so when I was four they took me and the kayak to Alaska to show me some of their favourite places.

They had a special dry suit made for me so that I would stay warm and dry in the cold wet weather and on the icy water near the glaciers. They found it impossible to measure me accurately because I wouldn't keep still and they got a different result each time. In the end they got me to lie down on a piece of paper, drew around me, cut the Kate shape out and posted it off to the manufacturers. Mum thought I looked like a little biker chick in my shiny black suit.

On our very first Alaskan kayaking journey we spent a few days at a place called Point Adolphus in South East Alaska. It is famous because humpback whales gather there to feed on krill, a tiny creature a little bit like plankton. As soon as we drifted out with the tide from the little beach where we had set up camp, we were surrounded by a group of whales surfacing, tail fluking, breaching and diving.

Finally the spectacular show ended and they slowly retreated into the distance blowing up huge plumes of spray as they swam. I was very quiet for a while. My parents mistook this for awestricken silence.

'Mum' I chirped eventually.

'Yes Kate' answered Mum expecting me to say something about the whales.

'Next time we go to a shop I really need to buy some pink nail varnish' I declared.

Despite my parents best efforts I was quite a normal little girl, keen on princesses, tiaras, pretty dresses and anything pink or sparkly. Unlike my Mum I didn't go through a George phase.

The whales made all kinds of strange noises. We could

hear them trumpeting like elephants, gurgling like drains and slapping their tails on the surface of the sea making a loud noise like a gun shot. Sometimes we could smell the fishy spray still lingering in the air.

At times it was possible to hear the whale song coming from underneath the surface of the water. Once Mum paddled out to sit with them and sing back to them. While she was out there she noticed that a big brown bear had appeared on the back of the beach where Dad and I were busy building sand castles. It was quite close to us but we hadn't noticed.

Mum started shouting and pointing and paddling towards us as fast as she could. When we finally heard her we both stood up and shouted back. This startled the bear which crashed away into the woods. Once we caught sight of the enormous grizzly, Dad and I both tried to jump into each other's arms at the same time.

In Alaska, to avoid attracting bears, we always had to do our cooking far away from the tent down by the sea so that any food smells could be washed away by the tide. This was quite tough when it was raining so hard that our food bowls were filling up with water faster than we could eat our meal or when there was no breeze and we had to walk up and down the beach as quickly as possible, shovelling mouthfuls of food under our bug nets and swatting the air with our spoons so the clouds of 'no see ums' and white socks couldn't inflict too much harm upon us while we ate.

Our food and cooking gear had to be hung up in bags between two trees. We had to remember not to store anything with a smell inside, even things like toothpaste. Mum has always worried because the dried meals that we ate gave us bad wind and our farts smelled exactly the same as the food which we had just eaten. What if the bears couldn't tell the difference between fart smells and real food and came to investigate? I always put Dad's smelly socks at the entrance of the tent to frighten away any unwanted visitors.

Sometimes the humpback whales swam really close to the shore, trawling along the kelp line with their huge mouths open.

We could see the nodules on their heads and the baleen plates in their jaws which they use to filter the seafood from the water. A group of sea lions also patrolled the kelp line. They followed our kayak very closely occasionally giving us a cheeky nudge.

Before we set out to Point Adolphus Mum had bought me a kids' fishing rod for $17 from the store at Hoonah. I don't think she had really expected me to catch anything with it so it was quite a shock when I hooked a king salmon on my very first attempt! It took all three of us to reel it in.

Icicle Bums and Grizzlies at Gloomy Knob

Glacier Bay, which was our next destination, is a National Park in the wilderness of South East Alaska, famous for its steep sided fjords and tide water glaciers, big frozen rivers of ice which wind their way down from the mountains to end in the ocean.

Sometimes the snout of a glacier is hundreds of feet high and several miles wide. When we approached them, we felt very tiny in our little red kayak looking up at the towering walls of ice with their prickly crowns of serac needles and deep blue chasms of crevasses.

It's not safe to paddle closer than half a mile because glaciers calve frequently, tons of ice crashing into the ocean with a thundering roar. It's not surprising that it was named 'White Thunder' by the Tlingit people who are native to this part of Alaska. A big calving can generate dangerous waves which could easily capsize a small boat.

Each calving leaves behind thousands of bergs floating on the water, fizzling and bubbling and chinking together like thousands of wind chimes. The icebergs are eroded by the waves to make very interesting shapes and often resemble other things such as swans, trees, boats and spooky castles. Dad and I made up stories together about them.

Mum wanted to take hundreds of pictures of me and Dad paddling amongst the icebergs. To be honest I got a bit fed up with it after a while and the only way Mum could get me to look and smile at the camera was sit in the water and shriek 'Ooh No I've got an icicle bum!' This never failed to amuse me. So if you like the photos of me and the icebergs spare a thought for my poor Mum and what she had to go through to get them!

It was fun weaving our way through the labyrinth of icebergs but we had to be careful that the passageways didn't close up behind us when the tide changed, leaving us trapped, or that we didn't rip the soft canvas of our folding boat on the sharp ice which sometimes protruded from the water like jagged shards of broken glass. Sometimes a gigantic berg would collapse or turn upside down next to us giving us a shock.

My favourite pastime in Glacier Bay was hunting for pretty shells. I spent hours beach combing for treasures to add to my collection. I also enjoyed gathering driftwood for our camp fire and harvesting the big, sweet wild strawberries which we found at the back of most beaches.

When the weather was wet and stormy we were stuck in the tent, sometimes for days at a time. Mum turned the tent into a pretend classroom and made up games to entertain me. The best one was when she drew out items from the supermarket, such as groceries and toiletries, for me to cut out, colour in and price, then we took it in turns to be shop keepers and customers using real American money to pay.

We spotted both black and brown bears in Glacier Bay. Bear attacks are extremely rare and mainly only happen if a bear has been provoked or feels threatened in some way but

we took a can of cayenne pepper spray with us just in case of an emergency.

One day, when Dad was pulling a bag out of the hatch, the nozzle of the bear spray got squashed and the pepper started spraying into the inside of the bag. Dad made the mistake of opening the bag and within seconds our eyes were streaming and our skin was on fire. Even after we moved away it was very painful. The pepper got onto a lot of our stuff and ruined it for further use as it was impossible to remove and continued to sting if you touched it.

Poor Dad fared the worst as he had opened the bag. He was almost blind and yelping with pain for over an hour. Trying to wash his face in the sea only made things worse. Using face wipes helped a bit and after a while he began to calm down. Mum got me settled into the tent. I was just beginning to drift off when there was another loud scream. Dad should have remembered to wash all the pepper spray off his hands before he went for a pee!

After three weeks of exploring the East and West Arms of the bay, we spent our final three days at a beach called Gloomy Knob because this is where the National Park boat 'The Spirit of Adventure' was scheduled to pick us up. Every evening, at the same time, a bear walked by, quite close to the tent. Each time it passed we all got into our kayak and paddled out onto the water to wait for it to leave just in case it became aggressive but the bear seemed oblivious to our presence.

On the last night we were sitting by our campfire when a big black shaggy wolf like the one in Little Red Riding Hood came out from the trees and stood still on the beach. After a few minutes it began to howl and its call was answered with a chorus of howls from the hillside above. On the same night we saw the Northern Lights: bright streaks of green and red flickering across the sky and we decided that my middle name should be Aurora.

On the day that we were due to be picked up, our bags of

gear were stacked in a neat pile next to the water's edge. We could hear the sound of the boat's engine in the distance, the volume gradually increasing.

'Well that's that!' said Mum. 'Surely nothing unexpected can happen now!'

I pointed up the hill and yelled 'Look Mum! It's that bear again!' At that moment the grizzly bear which had passed our tent earlier came crashing down the hillside and onto the far end of the beach before gradually making its way closer and closer to our spot, stopping every now and then to sniff at the ground.

The captain steered the boat right up to the beach, shouting to Dad to pass me up onto deck at once. They then proceeded to load up the rest of our gear in about two minutes flat before Mum and Dad climbed aboard, by which time the bear was just a few yards away, standing on its hind legs to scratch its back on a tree stump.

The tour guide told us that it was the closest grizzly sighting for the boat in years. All the passengers wanted to ask me questions and take my photo. I didn't mind because they kept presenting me with food that wasn't dehydrated or made from granola. The captain was so pleased with us for providing some entertainment that Mum and Dad were given a huge discount on their fare and I got to travel free!

The Upside Down Smelly Underpants Game

I was old enough to have my own little set of paddles the following year when we returned to South Central Alaska to explore Prince William Sound so I could join in when I wanted to. We all had to synchronise our paddling because the three seats were very close together. If anyone got slightly out of time our paddle blades clashed together and we all had to stop and begin again.

The first stage of the journey was from Valdez to Whittier.

Mum got a bit panicky when we were crossing the five mile wide Columbia Glacier. We had to navigate our way through a maze of icebergs, some bigger than a house. In addition to this there was a swell coming in from the outer coast causing the bergs to lurch up and down and smash together.

Sometimes when they toppled or collapsed it was too close for comfort and we felt very vulnerable in our little soft skinned kayak. The currents and tidal flows are complicated near the glacier and some bergs seemed to be drifting quickly towards us in one direction while others were moving the opposite way making us feel disorientated and slightly out of control.

We saw hundreds of sea otters. They are very different to the river otters which we see at home, also swimming in the sea. They are bigger and much furrier. They are very buoyant and usually float on their backs. They form big rafts together by linking paws.

The mothers carry their pups, also facing upwards on their tummies. I loved watching the mums teaching their squawking pups how to dive. When the otters are feeding they open the shellfish which they have caught by cracking them on their bellies, or by using their own special stone as a tool which they keep tucked away under their arms.

The pacific sea otters almost became extinct in the 18th and 19th centuries because they were hunted for their fur coats which are extremely thick. Fortunately they are now protected from commercial hunting and their numbers are increasing.

Now while I appreciate the fact that College Fjord, Harriman Fjord and Blackstone Bay were all very pretty with their snowy peaks and rainbow waterfalls cascading from toppling hanging glaciers etc, there is only so much of the scenery that a five year old can get excited about. I wasn't sleeping in the kayak as much as I did the year before therefore I needed to be entertained while my parents were admiring the lovely views. Mum sang songs with me and Dad told me stories which he made up as we paddled along. We all invented silly games.

My favourite game of all was the 'Smelly Underpants' game in which we took turns to think of the most ridiculous thing that we could imagine, upside down with smelly underpants on its head. It's simple! Here's an example. Imagine a drunken octopus wearing pink fluffy slippers and a curly wig, upside down with smelly underpants on its head. The others then have to laugh hysterically. Sometimes I insisted upon playing this game all day long.

I think my parents were relieved when we met two other kayakers called Ray and Deb to keep us company. We arrived one night in the dark at a place called Decision Point and were rustling around looking for a place to pitch the tent when a voice out of the alder bushes boomed 'Hey Bear! We looked up to see a man holding a rifle.

'Oh sorry I thought you were a bear! Come and join us' laughed Ray.

Our original plan had been to stay in Whittier while we stocked up with food for the next stage of the journey from Whittier to Seward. Ray and Deb invited us to stay with them in Anchorage instead. I had a blast. I made friends with the neighbours who had a giant paddling pool in their garden and I went to a birthday party at Chucky Cheese. Meanwhile the adults decided to team up for the next three weeks.

It was much more fun with Ray and Deb. Deb was really good at playing make believe games about princesses, weddings and shopping and she had a wash kit bag full of really interesting lotions and potions which she allowed me to play with. Mum's toilet bag consisted of a toothbrush and some wipes. Ray taught us different card and dice games. He also knew some great new songs. He brought along his travel guitar and fiddles for Mum and Deb to play so that every evening we had music around the campfire with me and Dad on percussion.

Another cool thing about Ray and Deb was their cooking tarp called a serendipity tent. There was room for the four of us to cook together away from the bugs and the rain while we told stories and played games.

Things were also looking up in the food department. Ray had his fishing gear with him and was an expert at using it so most nights we had salmon cooked on the fire, accompanied by chanterelles, chicken of the woods and sea greens. I loved helping Ray gut and fillet the fish though I wasn't keen on the lice which sometimes clung to the skin. They had room in their kayak for two boxes of wine which meant that Mum was happy.

We went for more hikes now there were four of us. Most hiking in Alaska involves a lot of bush whacking through tangled undergrowth and alder bushes or bog trotting through mud. We found one old path to an abandoned gold mine where we could see remains of the old machinery workings and mine shaft as well as the belongings of people who lived there around one hundred years ago.

The plan was to paddle to the south of the Sound then out into the Gulf of Alaska, rounding Cape Puget and Cape Resurrection to arrive at Seward in Resurrection Bay. After leaving Prince William Sound there is fifty miles of open ocean before entering the more sheltered waters of Resurrection Bay.

Our biggest adventure yet was when we left the protection of Port Bainbridge and hit a dense fog bank. Once we were enveloped by the mist we could see no further than a few yards. We could only see Ray and Deb if they paddled right next to us. Everything around us was white. The surface of the sea was glassy reflecting the blank white sky and it almost felt as if we were paddling through the air! It was a very surreal experience.

We had lost sight of the land because, although the surface of the sea was smooth there was a fairly big ground swell meaning that the surf was breaking heavily against the shore. We had to keep our distance from the coast to avoid being picked up and smashed onto the rocks. Paddling on a swell with no land in view was unnerving especially when, every now and then, without warning, a massive and invisible boomer of a wave exploded over submerged offshore rocks to either side of us.

Without any visible landmarks to guide them the grown ups had to rely on a map and compass for navigation. The roaring of the surf was a good indicator that we were going in the right direction but it was hard to tell how far we had gone. Then it began to go dark! We were scared.

To boost our morale we took turns to tell the others stories of the worst scrapes that we had ever been in. This was followed by accounts of our most embarrassing moments.
I was just introducing our friends to the smelly underpants game when Ray realised that the sound of the surf was gradually diminishing. To our great relief we had reached the entrance of Goat Harbour.

Unfortunately the only place we could find to land was on some tidal flats at the mouth of a big river where salmon were returning to their birthplace to spawn. Rotting fish carcasses and dying salmon were strewn across the gravel spit. There were signs of recent bear tracks and scat. In fact it was exactly the kind of place that campers are advised to avoid.

By now it was dark and we had no choice but to stay there. We pitched our tents close together and made three small fires around us. I constructed a 'bear scarecrow' from driftwood and the others took turns to keep a look out. There were no visitors, just a pack of coyotes howling in the woods.

Next morning we were glad that the mist had cleared because we still had another thirty miles of open ocean where any landing would be through dumping surf, not ideal for a folding kayak. After ten hours we were very happy to set foot on dry land especially the women who had not been able to pee into a bottle like the men, although we soon realised that there was no place to pitch a tent at Killer Bay, just a steeply sloping bank of large cobbles. The best we could do was to put up the cook tarp and all snuggle together until the morning.

As we paddled around the steep cliffs of Cape Resurrection, huge stacks and archways loomed above us through the mist and a big group of stellar sea lions, hauled out on a rock, groaned and belched above the spray.

By the time we got to Seward we had filled our water barrels with so many blueberries that we decided to make jam. Mum bought empty jars and sugar from the hardware store in town while the others set up a jam making station at the campsite using our Trangia and their MSR. Nobody can believe it when we tell them that we carried forty eight jars of homemade blueberry and wild strawberry jam back to Scotland in our hand luggage to give to our friends at Christmas but it's true!

The Boring Canyon

In 2005 we did three big trips. I was due to start school in 2006 and according to Mum and Dad we'd have to stick to going away in the holidays after that. As if!

In the autumn we flew to Las Vegas where we hired a car to transport our folding kayak to Lake Powell in Arizona. The Lake is really a part of the Colorado River. After the Glen Canyon Damn was built a big lake was created making it possible for people in boats to explore the steep, narrow, smooth sided canyons, sculpted from red desert rock, which snake out from the lake, winding around for miles. The canyons, with names like Labyrinth, Cathedral, Secret and Forbidding, are often hundreds of feet deep but only a few feet wide, with barely room to turn the kayak around.

We camped and swam from the sandy beaches, made giant sand castles with turrets and spikes and hiked up the twisted slot canyons where we came face to face with a rattlesnake!

Because nothing rots down in the desert, we had to hire a portable toilet to take in the kayak with us. After a while it smelled and made weird hissing, farting noises all the time.

After three weeks on the water we hired a car to go sight seeing around all the famous scenic areas such as Bryce, Zion, Monument Valley and the Grand Canyon. When we arrived at the rim of the Grand Canyon I refused to get out of the car.

'Not another boring canyon!' I grumbled. 'You go and look at it. I'll stay here in the car'

Shortly after that, sitting in the car at Arches National Park, waiting for the sun to set, I had a memorable light bulb moment. It finally dawned on me what 'I spy' was all about! We had been playing the game all week, Mum and Dad patiently taking turns to say 'I spy with my little eye something beginning with R' for example, to which I would happily guess away. 'Tree?' 'Car?' 'Snake?' and so on. As the light dimmed and the rocks of Window Arch began to turn a deep red I suddenly realised why Cloud begins with a C.

'I understand!' I yelled 'Cloud begins with C. Dog begins with D. Snake begins with S. Blow up the balloons. Let's have a party!'

It was a special occasion for us all. In fact we were far more excited about my 'I spy' revelation than we had been about the Grand Canyon which thereafter was always known to our family as 'The Boring Canyon!'

A River running through our Room

Phang Nga Bay in Thailand was where I overcame my fear of the water. All my friends loved the weekly toddler swimming lessons at the local pool and they splashed around happily, wearing their arm bands. For the first two years I clung

to Mum like a limpet, arms and legs wrapped around her tummy, refusing to let go of her, even though she took me every week until she began to despair. I even hated to get my face wet in the bath.

After I had learned to snorkel with flippers and mask and buoyancy aid, in the warm clear water above the coral reefs, teeming with brightly coloured tropical fish, I stopped feeling so afraid. Mum and I invented a make believe game about mermaids and by the end of the holiday I was swimming by myself.

We kayaked through tunnels and caves filled with stalactites into steep sided hongs where crab eating monkeys climbed down the jungle covered cliff sides. We explored mangrove swamps and camped on beaches with giant monitor lizards. Sometimes we bought fish and shrimps from the long tailed boats with their brightly coloured prayer flags.

My favourite memory of Thailand, apart from the great food, was camping out in a thunder storm when hundreds of lightning forks lit up the night sky and the rain was so powerful that we got out our shampoo and washed the salt out of our hair although we didn't like it when big rocks began to crash down from the overhanging cliff above, narrowly missing the tent.

Mum's favourite memory was also of a tropical storm. We were staying in a cheap hotel in Phuket. Grandad was in our room with us because the ceiling in his room was leaking. We were all lying together on one double bed and our bags were on the other because a river of rainwater was pouring in through one door, underneath both beds and out through the bathroom. The power was off so it was dark apart from the frequent flashes of lightning.

Eventually the grown ups nodded off but I was too excited and had invented a game where I was a poor, ill treated maid like Cinderella. Mum said she woke up at 3 o clock in the morning when the lights came back on to see me dressed in a cloak and shawl which I had made from towels, twirling around the room, sweeping the floor with a besom broom and humming to myself!

A Trail of Fairy Houses

Our very last trip ever, supposedly, was a six month, 1200 mile sea kayaking journey from Vancouver to Glacier Bay, through the Inside Passage of British Columbia and South East Alaska.

We took Ducky on the back of the kayak with us as usual. He is a yellow plastic duck who has been our mascot ever since he found Mum and Dad one day when they were kayaking in Scotland. They had been sitting on a beach near Ullapool when they saw a plastic duck bobbing up to the water's edge. He had the number 124 on the bottom. They picked him up and set him afloat. Two days later they were sitting eating chips on the dock in Lochinver when another yellow duck floated in. He had the same number underneath! He had followed them on the wind and tide for thirty miles. Since then Ducky has joined them on all their adventures at sea and survived, even when an amorous blue jay attempted to mate with him.

Despite our good luck duck there were some long spells of bad weather that summer and a fair number of our days were spent stormbound on beaches, miles from civilisation, our food supplies dwindling as we waited for the winds to calm down.

In fact we were forced to stop paddling and set up camp after the first two miles of day one by gale force headwinds although this wasn't in the wilderness. It was in the centre of Vancouver, surrounded by skyscrapers and office blocks. In the evening we managed to struggle across to a city park on the north side of town, where we hid our tent behind

some bushes out of view of the floodlights and No Camping signs.

Whenever the northwesterlies blew up and prevented further progress, I busied myself with my latest project which was building fairy houses out of stones, leaves and driftwood. We always practise 'no trace camping', trying to leave each place exactly as we found it but, this year, anyone following behind us would have been able to track our route from the trail of miniature houses left behind on the beaches.

It was a challenge to find places to camp on the coast of BC. The shoreline is steep and rocky and the vegetation of the temperate rainforest is very dense and tangled, the branches of the crowded spruce and hemlock sprouting out of the trunks all the way down to ground level.

Spots to pitch a tent were few and far between. Sometimes we were paddling late in the evening and still hadn't found anywhere suitable. Once we had to camp on a rickety floating raft that had been left anchored out from an abandoned fish farm. In the night the wind blew up and the raft began to lurch and sway on the waves, tossing us up and down in the tent. At least we didn't have to think about hanging our food out of reach of the bears that night.

We were sure we had discovered the perfect location one evening when we pulled up on the shore of a tiny grass covered islet with a flat spot on the top just big enough for the three of us. What we hadn't accounted for was the very high spring tide. By midnight the whole island had disappeared beneath the sea apart from the patch where our tent was and about two inches of grass all the way round it.

In the Copeland Islands at the northern tip of the Sunshine Coast we found a beautiful sandy beach. We shared it with another camper who was travelling around BC recording signs or sightings of Big Foot or Sasquatch.

By all accounts there had been plenty of activity the night before on that very island including a large, shadowy, two legged being crashing through the woods and huge footprints left behind on the sand in the morning. Fortunately our night on the island was uneventful, much to my relief and Mum's disappointment.

After the town of Lund the highway on the mainland ends and we didn't meet another road head until we arrived at Prince Rupert six hundred miles away. From here the only way through the archipelagos of forested islands, most of which are uninhabited, is by boat.

For us that meant as much as three weeks of paddling between the tiny coastal villages where we could buy supplies so we had to pack enough food and fuel to be self sufficient for that time.

There are many narrow channels passing between the myriads of islands along the coast. Whichever route we chose Mum had to be very precise with tidal planning because dangerous tidal rapids run through the narrow sections, sometimes reaching speeds of sixteen knots.

As the current approaches the middle of its flood or ebb, the water becomes a maelstrom of whirlpools, boils and waterfalls, hazardous to small boats, especially to a little, fully laden kayak carrying a family, their home and all their belongings. Mum had to use the Canadian tide and current tables to predict the exact time of slack water for navigating the Yukulta, Devil's Hole, Whirlpool and Green Point Rapids.

Even then the water felt swirly and oily as if we were sneaking over the back of a sleeping monster which could wake up in a furious rage at any time. From our camp on Stuart Island at night we could hear its thunderous roar from over a mile away.

In the Broughton Archipelago we passed the clamshell middens, old long houses and totem poles of villages where the First Nation people of this area once lived such as Mamaliliculla on Village Island. Nearby at the thriving community of Alert Bay we saw more recent carvings

including the world's tallest totem pole and we visited the Namgis Big House where traditional dances are performed by the T'sasala Cultural Group and important ceremonies such as the Potlatch are held.

After Port Hardy we left the protection of Vancouver Island and paddled along the outer coast of Queen Charlotte Sound, where, for the next fifty miles, we were exposed to the open Pacific. Mum and Dad were nervous about approaching Cape Caution with its reputation of very turbulent seas near the point, especially as we would be paddling close to the place where the infamous Nakwakto Rapids rage through Slingsby Channel.

The race through these narrows is so violent that nearby Tremble Island actually shakes. If the ebb tide, the speed of which has been known to reach eighteen miles per hour, meets an incoming westerly sea, this area is not a good place to be caught out in a kayak

While we were waiting for calmer conditions we passed the time beach combing at Allison Harbour and we found some of the small glass blue and orange trading beads exchanged by the European traders for furs and the beautiful craftwork made by the people who once lived here. These beads were used by explorers like Captain Cook over three hundred years ago. It was very exciting when we actually found one, a bit like discovering real treasure.

Along the outside coast camping was easy for a change with pristine sandy beaches covered with driftwood and patterned with the prints of deer, wolves and bears.

In BC the weather was mainly dry and sunny but our progress was often hindered by the strong north westerly headwinds. Often the only way to avoid the winds was to make a very early start, getting onto the water at first light to take advantage of the brief period of calm.

To make it easier for me, Mum and Dad used to pack everything into the dry bags and load the kayaks, leaving me

curled up asleep in my sleeping bag until the very last minute. Sometimes they even managed to get my kayaking gear on and gently bundle me into my seat without disturbing me, handing me a Snickers bar for breakfast when I woke up.

In Alaska the winds turned to the south east which was in our favour but instead we had almost six weeks of consistent rain or 'liquid sunshine' as the locals call it. Camping was tough in these conditions because we never got the chance to dry anything out. We had to put on soggy kayaking gear in the morning and even our dry clothes and sleeping bags felt permanently damp and claggy.

We kept to our rule of cooking and eating away from the tent but a mealtime in the rain, with the hoards of biting insects, was a miserable experience and we tried to get it over with as fast as possible.

The most challenging thing about paddling in these conditions was trying to find our way in the fog. A lot of the coast here looks identical, just trees and water for miles and we had some big crossings to make such as Frederick Sound which is thirteen miles wide. All we had was a compass and a map and Mum was worried that when we arrived on the other side we wouldn't know where we were. Crossing the mouth of the Stikine River with its complicated tidal currents, in zero visibility was nerve racking, particularly when our kayak became grounded on a shoal of quicksand in the middle of the channel.

After days of wearing wet gear it's not surprising that coming across a natural hot spring was a huge treat for us. Soothing our smelly, sore, shivering bodies in a bath of hot water was absolutely blissful even if the water did smell a little bit eggy.

Our favourite hot spring was at Baranof. There were three tubs down at the dock and a small café where we could drink hot chocolate, play cards and chat to other travellers. Behind the village a trail led up into the woods where a rocky pool

was situated on the edge of a river gorge so we could relax in the warm water and feel the cool spray from the waterfall on our faces.

Apart from the occasional fishing boat in the distance we went for days without seeing a soul but the people we did meet along the way were so kind and hospitable. Whenever we arrived at a village we were invited into people's homes or holiday cabins or welcomed aboard people's boats.

We were surprised how many people had already heard about our journey, greeting us with 'Oh you must be the mad kayaking family from Scotland!'

When we arrived at Anan Creek near Wrangell, we thought that we would just have to make a flying visit to the bear observatory there because camping is forbidden in the area due to the high density of bears. Luckily we met a lovely lady called Karla who was travelling the coast of South East Alaska in a rowing boat and she invited us to stay in the Forestry cabin that she was renting for a few days.

It was the middle of the summer season and the river was so fully packed with writhing jostling pink salmon that it looked like a huge boiling pot of fish soup. Bald eagles were perched in the trees above and bears were spread out across the rocks, swiping at their prey or feasting on their catch.

When there is such an abundance of food, the bears often only eat the parts of the body which are rich in nutrients and energy such as the eyes and brains, leaving the rest to rot in the sunshine. The smell got pretty ripe at times. Although it made a pleasant change to eat inside the cabin it was a shame that Mum had chosen canned pink salmon as the protein element of our evening meal for two nights that week!

One morning on the way up to the viewing platform we came face to face with a bear standing in the middle of the trail. It was huffing and swinging its head from side to side

which was a sign that it was annoyed and might be about to charge.

Following the advice which we had been given we said 'Hey Bear!' loudly and clapped our hands so that the bear would know that we were humans. It's not a good idea to run from a bear as this is more likely to make them want to chase you and they can run MUCH faster than people! We stood our ground and kept on talking and it was a relief when the bear eventually turned round and left the trail.

At Tenakee we stayed with our new friends Pat and Teri in their summer house in Tenakee. While they were giving us a ride down Tenakee Inlet on their skiff we saw something which we had never seen before. Suddenly, without warning six or seven gigantic mouths burst out of the still water just a few metres away from our boat!

A group of humpback whales were bubblenet feeding. The whales dive together to form a group and start blowing bubbles. The bubbles form a kind of trap in which small fish like herring become stunned and confused. When enough food has been captured within the net of bubbles the whales all swim to the surface together with their jaws wide open to swallow their prey. We saw it happen four more times as we cruised down the inlet.

Our final destination was McBride Glacier in Glacier Bay. We arrived there in September when the first flakes of snow were beginning to fall after spending a month in Gustavus with our friend Vince, living in a tree house in his garden, while Dad got a job helping to build a house next door to fund our ferry journey back to Vancouver.

When we had passed through Johnstone Strait, between Vancouver Island and the mainland, the resident pods of orca whales for which the area is famous, had not yet arrived as it was too early in the year. The following year we returned to Telegraph Cove and paddled to Kaikash Creek for a week to watch the pods of orcas swimming past. They often surfaced next to our kayak. We were even lucky enough to observe mothers and calves swimming right up to the shore to scratch their bellies on the cobbles.

The whales were late arriving that year so we changed our return flight to two weeks later meaning that I was a fortnight late for my second year at school. When Dad phoned to explain, Mr Earnshaw the headmaster said that camping on a beach waiting for orca whales to appear had to be the most original excuse for being absent from school that anyone had ever given!

CHAPTER 3

CYCLING CANADA

A Nice Normal Family

For my Mum's last birthday her friend gave her a glass plaque engraved with the words 'As far as anyone knows we are just a nice normal family'. It always makes us giggle.

You can spot our family a mile off at the airport. We're the ones wearing four sets of clothes each, a woolly hat, wellington boots and sunglasses. You can see us sweating beneath layer upon layer of thermal underwear, fleece tops, down jackets and waterproofs even though it's mid July and not raining. Our luggage which usually includes a kayak or two, amongst other things, causes a major obstruction at the check in queue.

Because the 'holidays' we go in for usually require us to bring our own bedroom, kitchen and chosen mode of transport with us, we inevitably struggle to stay within the baggage allowance weight limit. Mum, however, has come up with an ingenious solution. The best way to reduce the size and weight of our bags is to wear absolutely everything which can be worn. After all there are no restrictions applied to the size and weight of the passengers themselves.

As we wobble and shuffle our overloaded trolleys with

their oversized, odd shaped cargo towards the desk, Mum and Dad anxiously scan the faces of the officials who are about to deal with us to try and determine which one of them is of the most sympathetic disposition.

'Look your cutest Kate' Mum whispers to me. To Dad she mutters between clenched teeth 'Smile and remember we're just a nice normal family going on a nice normal holiday!'

The spring of 2009 was no exception except in the place of folding kayaks we had a tandem, a single bike and two bob trailers. These had been boxed up in such a way that it appeared as if we were carrying a double and single bed in our luggage.

Of all the Famous Five stories Mum's favourite was 'Five get into Trouble' where the children head off into the English countryside on their bikes, sleeping beneath the stars, swimming in ponds and calling at lonely farmhouses to buy fresh eggs and ice creams, all washed down with lashings of ginger beer. Eventually one of the children is kidnapped by a ruffian named Rooky and taken to a mysterious mansion called 'Owl's Dene.' When the others go to the rescue, they too are taken captive until they come up with the plan of hiding the youngest boy in the back of Mr. Perton's black Bentley before he drives into town so that, when the opportunity arises, he can jump out and fetch the police. Meanwhile Julian discovers a secret room behind a bookshelf where an escaped convict is hiding with a handkerchief full of stolen diamonds.

According to Mum life just doesn't get any better than that. From the moment she read this novel she daydreamed about setting off down the dappled country lanes, with a couple of like minded friends, into the unknown, in search of adventure. She didn't realise that it would be over thirty years before she actually did just that, that the couple of like minded friends would be her long suffering husband and daughter, or that the journey into the unknown would take us 16,500 miles from Arctic Canada to Southern Patagonia.

Although, as Dad helpfully pointed out, having read the warning sections on some of the countries that we would be passing through, her childhood fantasy of being kidnapped by villains would finally stand a pretty good chance of coming true!

I was eight years old and my parents had decided that if they were going to take me out of school for a long adventure, then this was the time to do it. They had some money saved from a good run of tree planting contracts and their friend was looking for a place to rent. Mum's teaching experience (before she decided that she preferred trees to children) was with eight to ten year olds so she figured that she could probably manage to home educate me over that stage of my life.

They also, correctly, assumed that when I became a teenager at high school, my social life would become a bigger priority and I would be reluctant to leave my friends for long periods of time.

Looking back I don't think I fully understood the concept of leaving home to travel the world for two years. The reality of it only really dawned on me after the first year. I didn't question the fact that my parents, who had no previous cycling touring experience, had planned their journey using an atlas that was twenty years out of date. At that age I just accepted whatever my parents planned for me.

I mean grown ups are sensible and always know what they are doing, right?

A very STEEP Learning Curve

Here's the thing. My parents knew absolutely nothing at all about cycling when they dreamt up this latest scheme. Apart from me, nobody in our family even owned a bike. I mean we all knew how to ride one (although I couldn't help

wondering a few times in the earlier stages of the trip how long ago Mum's stabilizers had been taken off). What they hadn't done was any cycle touring – not one single overnight trip where they had to carry camping gear. They certainly had never pulled trailers or ridden with pannier bags.

Our only experience of riding on unpaved roads was a Sunday afternoon on the forestry tracks of Grizedale Sculpture Park.

There was no need to worry though. Their plan was to finish work a month before we left Britain. They would practise packing up the panniers and trailers with everything that we would need as well as getting the hang of cycling with loaded bikes.

The reality was a different story. They were still rushing around trying to finish a tree planting contract four days before we left for Canada. The new bikes and trailers never even got taken out of their boxes until we disembarked at Inuvik in the North West territories of Canada.

When we arrived it was raining and the air outside was thick with bloodthirsty mosquitoes. The airport was due to close in an hour so the trailers needed to be assembled and attached to the bikes which then had to be packed, preferably while we were still inside. It was not a good time to discover that there wasn't nearly enough room for all the stuff we had brought. Even after donating our holdalls and rucksack to the airport lost property the trailers were hopelessly overloaded.

It was a ten mile ride to the campsite in the centre of town, also not a good time for Mum to find out that she couldn't ride a bike and pull a trailer at the same time. For the first few miles she just wobbled all over the road and fell off yelling 'There is absolutely no way I'll ever get the hang of this!'

The trailer had a habit of parking itself whenever she slowed down or hesitated. A month into the trip we met another cyclist with a trailer who showed her the easy way to park the bike and trailer against one another and, even more importantly, the technique of lifting them back up again. Until then poor Dad had to prop the tandem on its bike stand, leaving me to hold it steady, while he helped her lift the whole rig up again. This must have happened about thirty times on the short ride into town. What was worrying was that we still had two weeks of food to add to the load and we hadn't even left the tarmac yet!

Inuvik is in the Arctic Circle, about fifty miles from the Arctic Ocean. In summer the sun doesn't set. It was still shining brightly at midnight and children were playing ball in the streets at 1am.

We spent three days there, trying to work out what items we could manage without and giving away at least half our clothes to other campers. Our gear wasn't very lightweight because, on the whole, we were using the same equipment that we had used on our kayaking trips.

Also because of my age I think that we had more belongings than the average cycle tourist. Unlike my parents who took two sets of clothes for two years, one to wear and one to wash, I insisted upon bringing a selection of non hideous clothes in my Ortlieb crafted wardrobe. In addition to this the trailer was full of toys, art material and books for my home education. (My parents who are dinosaurs had yet to find out about things like Kindles or educational software.)

At one point in the journey we were carrying five teddies, three Bratz dolls, two Sylvanian Families plus furniture, a violin, a portable DVD player and a miniature pool table!

We had to stock up with enough food for three weeks because after the first hundred miles there would be no villages or shops for another four hundred miles. Half of our food was stuffed inside two bear proof barrels inside the pannier bags. A couple on the campsite where we were staying were heading south in their RV and they offered to drop our rations for the second two weeks at Eagle Plains, an isolated

51

hotel half way along the Dempster Highway meaning that we wouldn't need to carry so much.

The grocery store is expensive in Inuvik because the supplies have to be flown in. Fresh produce costs the most because it is heavy and cannot be stored for long. A carton of milk cost us eleven dollars!

Some friendly locals showed us around the community greenhouse, under a huge glass dome, where people can grow their own vegetables, making the most of the long daylight hours during the summer.

The Dempster Highway is almost five hundred miles long. It is very rough in places with thick, loose gravel, big chunks of rock, cracks and potholes. It was featured on the 'Ice Road Truckers' series, a famous documentary following the lives of people who drive their huge lorries across the frozen arctic in the middle of winter to take supplies to remote gas fields and mines in the far North.

On the small plane from Whitehorse to Inuvik Mum had got chatting to a resident of the town who had managed to convince her we were all making a terrible mistake by the time she had finished her complimentary pretzels and orange juice.

'Are you completely out of your minds?' he said 'Nobody cycles the Dempster! It's bad enough in a car. It's like the surface of Mars! The gravel's so deep you'll just sink!' He shook his head. 'And what about all those great big trucks' he added. 'Thundering past all the time kicking up rocks in your faces the size of pumpkins. They can't stop you know! And may the lord help you if it rains!' He sighed dramatically. 'You'll never make it!'

Not particularly encouraging news. After four days in Inuvik, Mum had yet to manage a full circuit of the campsite without falling off.

Apart from a half hour tandem lesson from the staff at JD Cycles in Yorkshire, Dad and I hadn't had much practice at cycling a bicycle made for two either. When we finally left town and rode onto the beginning of the long dirt road, right next to the sign which says 'Dawson City 767km', all three of us keeled over and crashed to the ground simultaneously. Not a very good start.

Our trailers and bikes were heavy and we found them very unstable to begin with, especially poor Mum who spent more time pushing her bike than riding it. Dad remarked, unhelpfully, that she might as well have put all her gear in a wheelbarrow and just pushed that instead.

We had hoped to cycle about thirty miles a day but, to begin with, we were lucky if we managed twenty.

The road was extremely dusty. It was easy to see why all the cars in Inuvik are brown, even the ones which are supposed to be white. Whenever a truck was coming we could see a cloud of dust getting closer like the approach of a steam train. We had to stop pedalling and turn our faces away from the road, shielding ourselves so that we didn't get hit by flying pieces of gravel. Once a truck had passed it took a while for the air to clear enough for us to be able to see where we were going.

The drivers were very considerate towards us. They tried their best to slow down when they saw us. Sometimes they even passed food and water down to us from their cabs.

The first few days were exhausting. The Arctic is actually pretty warm in the summer. There is twenty four hours of sunlight and the small scrubby trees provide little shade so the inside of the tent was like a sauna day and night, making it difficult to get any rest.

Outside we had to wear our bug jackets the whole of the time, even when cycling, because we were covered from head to toe with big biting mosquitoes. We felt quite claustrophobic, lying inside the tent, hearing their loud, high pitched whining and seeing them in their hundreds, squatting against the mesh, waiting for someone to come out.

They knew it was only a matter of time before someone

would need the toilet and they would get to feast on bare flesh. Peeing while smacking our legs and bottom frantically to try and prevent any insects landing wasn't much fun. We also had to perfect the art of entering and exiting the tent by only opening up the tiniest gap for the shortest time possible so that the hoards poised at the entrance didn't all zoom into the tent. One of us would open the zip while the person coming in or out dived through the space a bit like a seal or acrobat jumping through a hoop.

Most of the time, we were sweaty, tired, bruised, and itching from our bites. Our bottoms were sore and our legs aching from using new muscles.

After three days we had to ride our bikes onto a ferry to cross the Mackenzie River, the biggest in Canada. In the winter months the river freezes and people just drive over it. In the spring and autumn, during the times when the ice is breaking up and re-forming, the river cannot be crossed. Apparently there were big chunks of ice flowing downstream just two weeks before we arrived and the ferry had only been running for a week.

There were many fish camps here where people were drying whitefish on racks and smoking them over a fire. We bought a bag of dried fish strips which were chewy and salty, a bit like jerky.

We were given a very friendly welcome by Melissa and Kurt who ran the Tsiigehtchic band store. Their son Christopher was the same age as me. They took us into their home, cooked us meals, washed our grubby clothes and sent us away with a bag of goodies.

One thing that we did not want to have to deal with on the Dempster Highway was wet weather. Everyone said that if there was continuous heavy rain, the road would turn into a mud bath for weeks. It would be impossible to cycle through the thick slush and the grit would totally wreck our bikes.

Fortunately there was only three days of rain. A Gwich'in

family invited us to stay with us during that time. Gwich'in is the name of the First Nation people who live in this area. When we first arrived in Fort McPherson, late in the evening after a long and gruelling day on the gravel, a lady called Rosemary spotted us from her car, looking for a place to camp. It had started to rain and the mosquitoes were particularly fierce. She offered us a room in her house. She had to go out to her job in a restaurant shortly but she told us to make ourselves at home.

She came back a few hours later bringing a bag full of hot food from work to share with us. After we had eaten she called her daughter and told her to bring her nine year old daughter, Angel to come and play with me. Mum couldn't help laughing because it was about one o clock in the morning! When it stays light all the time and the children are on holiday, nobody takes much notice of the time. People just sleep when they feel like it.

In winter it is dark for twenty four hours a day. The people go out on skidoos and dog sleds and camp out on the ice. We were given some Arctic sea trout which had been caught from a hole drilled in the ice. We also tried caribou meat which reminded me of venison.

The Gwich'in women are well known for their beautiful bead work. Rosemary showed us an intricate shawl which she had been working on for her two year old grandson.

Our first hundred miles had been flat and vegetated with small spruce and birch trees known as boreal forest. After Fort McPherson we began to climb up into the tundra where there are no trees although there are plenty of flowers. The ground beneath the tundra is always frozen, even in summer which is why they call it permafrost.

At the Arctic Circle viewpoint at 66 degrees north we saw lots of inukshuks. These are little stone figures. In the past the Gwich'in people used them to communicate and give directions to each other when they were following the migrating caribou herds. They are quite easy to make. I made one myself.

The caribou hunt still plays an integral part in the lives of the Gwich'in people today. The meat is an important part of their diet and the hides are still used to make shoes and clothing. When we got to the top of Windy Pass I found some old caribou hides which had been left behind from a camp. I really wanted to take one with us to make things with but Mum said that they had lice in them.

The gravel around here was terrible! Apparently the Inuit people have over one hundred words for snow. It wouldn't surprise me if the people here have that many different words for gravel as well! One day, after pushing our bikes for hours up a seven mile long hill, Mum found that she had to push hers all the way back down the other side because she couldn't keep her balance on the large loose stones.

At other times there was less gravel but the road was hard and crumpled like a corrugated tin roof. This type of surface is known as washboard and is incredibly bumpy. Dad had deliberately chosen bikes without suspension because there are fewer parts to go wrong, but we could have really done with it here! The vibrations shook through our bodies and I was sure I could feel my teeth rattling and my brain sloshing around inside my skull. Our bottoms were also in a sorry state.

Because of the permafrost and the extreme winter conditions, causing the surface to crack, the road is constantly under construction. One evening we pitched our tent outside a construction camp where the workers live during the week. The staff were concerned about us because a grizzly had been sighted recently, prowling close to the buildings. They invited us to sleep inside and the three of us were let loose in the staff canteen to feast on hot dinners with chips and gravy and puddings with ice cream until we could eat no more.

We had to carry food for several days on this stretch of

road so every little bite was rationed out. One day Mum and Dad had a massive fight when Dad caught Mum sneakily nibbling off a corner of the sacred cheese block while she was cooking. I sometimes think if the 'Hunger Games' was a real event I'd be in with a chance of winning. After all I seem to have been in training for it for most of my life!

Between Fort McPherson and Dawson City there are four hundred miles of empty road with no villages, shops or houses of any kind. The only exception to this is Eagle Plains. The sign there says 'Eagle Plains Population 6'

The hotel where our supplies had been dropped was here. We were hot, tired, sore and filthy when we arrived. We parked our bikes next to a truck painted with the words 'Have Truck, Will Gravel' (instead of Have Kids, Will Travel) and went in to ask if we could camp outside. At the desk we got the most wonderful surprise. Brad, a motorcyclist who had stopped to chat with us twice on his way to Inuvik and back, had paid for a room for us at the hotel! There was no way that we could have afforded to stay in a hotel while we were in Canada on a budget of £20 day for all three of us. Mum was quite tearful and overwhelmed at this act of kindness. A soft comfortable bed away from the constant mosquitoes and a bath to soothe our achy, itchy, dirty bodies was a blissful treat.

It was one of many memorable acts of generosity and hospitality that we experienced from strangers on our journey. Over the two years people who had only just met us offered us places to stay, shared their food, gave us money to help fund our days on the road and helped with bike repairs amongst other things. The trip would have been much tougher and a lot less fun without their company and friendship.

There were four wilderness campgrounds along the highway. They always had a shelter with mosquito proof mesh windows and tables. This was a good place for me to get some school work done. Mum tried to do an hour of English and Maths with me every day while Dad serviced the bikes.

I had some workbooks with stickers which were all about a wizard called Whimstaff, his apprentice Pointy and his two lazy frog servants, Muggly and Buggly. They had names like 'Magical Multiplication' and 'Mysterious Maths'

I also wrote a diary about all the different things I saw and learned about on my journey. This included little history and geography projects related to the areas through which we passed. Mum emailed the journal back to my class teacher every month to read out to my class and they sometimes emailed me back to let me know what things they had been learning. The journal that I wrote formed the basis for this book because my parents were too lazy to write their own.

Dad practised my times tables with me as we were cycling along and when I got older Mum got me to use my maths skills to work out the answers to questions related to our trip such as speed, distance, times, converting kilometres to miles and the costs of things in different currency.

In one of these campgrounds we met a biologist called Carissa. She was carrying out scientific research on the tundra here and she was known as 'The Dempster Girl' She had her fiddle with her and she taught me how to play 'Boil those Cabbages Down' on my violin while her Dad who we called 'Sourdough Mac' made sourdough bread for us on the top of the wood burning stove.

At Tombstone Campground Igor, a local photographer drove us out to a fox den site where we could watch the mothers with their kits, playing, jumping and rolling around on the grass. Most were red but some had black stripes and a white tip on their tail. When they had disappeared into their holes Igor took us up to Three Moose Lake where we watched a big bull moose diving for sweet grass growing under the water on the lake's bed.

After a month the big day finally came when we cycled off the gravel and onto smooth hard tarmac. Cycling on a paved road was completely different. We were now easily able to cover forty miles a day although, according to Dad, I kept jumping off the bike every five minutes to rescue every single little slug or insect which I saw crossing the road. I couldn't bear to think of them getting squashed by the next car.

It doesn't take our family long to start turning feral when we are camping. By the time two days have passed we are usually growling at each other and fighting over food. After almost three weeks in the wilderness my parents had to be slowly integrated back into civilization. For example I had to remind Mum that it was no longer socially appropriate to just squat down and pee wherever she felt like it now that we were in a town, albeit a small and sparsely populated one, and that, just because the mosquitoes of the Yukon found her bare bottom a joy to behold, it didn't mean that the residents of Dawson City would feel the same way.

We stocked up with a week of supplies in Dawson City. Although we now had a paved road there were still big distances between villages and stores.

There was a famous gold rush here over a hundred years ago. We visited a museum where we learned how people from all over America left their homes and took a long and dangerous journey in the hope of finding their fortune. After sailing up the Inside Passage of BC and Alaska they had to carry 1000kg of belongings over a high snowy mountain pass known as the Chilkoot Trail before building rafts to travel up the Yukon River in order to stake a claim. Many people died on the way and for those who made it living conditions were very harsh.

Small amounts of gold can still be found in the rivers here. In town I went for a lesson on how to pan for gold and found six small specks. Dad bought me my own small pan and we tried panning as we cycled along the banks of the Yukon but we never got rich.

There were hundreds of juicy wild strawberries on the side of the road. Some were as big as my thumbnail and we

often stopped to pick them. We weren't the only ones! Bears love to eat berries. We had been so busy stuffing our faces that we only realised that a grizzly had also been feasting a few metres away on the other side of a bush. Once a bear ran alongside our bikes for a while and we couldn't tell whether it was chasing after us or running away!

In the Yukon there was a Forestry campground about every forty miles which was ideal for us. They were very basic with just a water tap and fire pits and an honesty box into which we put our fee of about £5 a night.

Because it was summer the campsites were full of families from the towns having a holiday. We were invited to lots of barbecues for meals and I was never short of kids to play with.

There were also plenty of retired couples in campervans or RVs as they are known in Canada. They usually had a cute little dog which I would make a fuss of and ask questions about. Then if food was cooking I would sniff the air and say 'Mmmmmm! That smells much nicer than what we're having. What is it?' This shameless strategy often resulted in me or the whole family being invited into a campervan for dinner.

Otter's Adventure

A terrible thing happened while we were staying on one of these campgrounds. Mum and I had gone for a walk around and after playing on the swings I noticed that Otter wasn't with me. Otter is the very first teddy that I really bonded with. I got her when we were kayaking in Prince William Sound at the age of four and she has been with me on all my travels. Since we left Scotland I carried her with me all the time, even on the bike so I must have dropped her somewhere along the trail. We retraced our steps but she was nowhere to be seen.

We searched the whole campsite but still couldn't find her.

Dad went around and asked all the campers for help and got in contact with the warden. Mum made 'Missing' posters with a picture of Otter which they stuck to the notice boards.

On his search Dad spoke to a lady who told him that she had found her on the ground and had put her next to the gate at the entrance to the site but when we went to look she had disappeared. Someone must have taken her.

Next morning we had to leave without her. We were all very sad. In fact we were so heartbroken that we felt like going home. I couldn't help wondering what had happened to her and if she was lost and lonely without me.

At the next campground we had two visitors, a kind Swiss couple who had heard our story and driven their RV forty miles down the road especially to give me their own teddy bear, Floppy, to try to cheer me up because they felt so sorry for me. It was very sweet of them but I still felt terribly sad. Floppy was beautiful but I wasn't ready for him to take the place of my beloved Otter. It didn't feel right.

I couldn't sleep so Mum and I went for a walk down to the lake, built a little fire and stayed there until the sun set. As we were making our way back along the little forest trail Mum suddenly screamed 'KATE LOOK!' Soon I was shrieking for joy as well for there, sitting on a tree stump in the middle of nowhere, in the far corner of the campground, forty miles away from where we had lost her, was Otter!

Dad said that when he heard all the yelling he thought that we must have been attacked by a bear and came running down the track with the cayenne pepper spray in his hand.

If we hadn't decided to go for a walk down to the lake that night we would have left the campsite next day without ever knowing that she was there. How she found her way back to us remains a mystery. If only she could talk we might have been able to tell the story of her adventure.

Now there were two teddy bears on a tandem.

The Rabid Grizzly

Whitehorse with a population of around 27,000 is the biggest town in the Yukon. We were very excited to spot our first supermarket in weeks. It had more than one aisle!

Many people assume that long distance cycle touring is all about having adventures in exotic places with incredible scenery, wildlife and unfamiliar cultures. Well that does come into it every now and then but the truth is that most of our lives seemed to revolve around buying food for the next stretch of road and packing things into and out of bags. I can tell you that a large portion of my ninth, tenth and eleventh years was spent sitting outside shops while Mum and Dad wrestled with boxes, tubes, cans, bars, Ziploc bags and barrels.

Fortunately Mum loves arranging things into dry bags. It is her hobby. Traditionally normal women are supposed to have a thing about shoes and handbags. They just can't help wanting them when they see them whether they need them or not!

My mother is not one of those women. Let's face it. Who needs high heeled shoes and a designer handbag when you can wear socks with sandals along with a huge red bum bag with twenty compartments and room for an ice axe, like she does?

However if she sees a waterproof dry bag in a new colour or design she wants it and will invent a special reason for it's use, sometimes even a whole expedition, just so she can justify buying it. With her it's not Gucci or Versace that gets her drooling, it's Ortlieb or Palm.

Mum's favourite form of evening relaxation was to play with her dry bags, rearranging the contents and devising new ways of improving upon the existing packing system. Dad and I were never quite able to keep up with the frequent changes and consequently struggled with finding our belongings. Mum would then become irritable about the fact that she was the only one of us who ever knew where anything was stored.

While we were staying on the camp site in town we woke up in the middle of the night and noticed that the sky was dark and we could actually see the stars for the first time.

It was a hot summer in the Yukon and there were some enormous forest fires. On one day there were over forty fires in the area near us. The air was often thick with smoke and there was a layer of ash on our tent in the morning. We could see big billowing grey clouds tinged with flame behind the hills. On the news there were warnings of the possibilities of road closures and people having to evacuate their homes.

Forest fires are common in the summer. As we cycled along the Klondike Highway we passed mile after mile of charred black forest. It isn't long before new life springs up in the form of fireweed, its bright pink flowers forming a haze of colour between the dead tree stumps.

We stopped at a café which was famous for having the worlds' biggest cinnamon buns. They had a diameter of twenty centimetres. We bought one and divided it between the three of us like a pizza.

At Watson Lake we went to see the biggest signpost forest on the planet. It has 53,000 signs brought there by travellers from all over the world. It was the size of a small town. I made my own sign saying 'Kate 8 Cycling from Inuvik to South America'

Although we hardly ever saw a shop we had been having difficulty staying within our budget so Mum decided that, in order to save money, we should make more effort to look for places to wild camp. One night we camped at a rest area called 'The Rabid Grizzly Recreation Park'. I was woken up in the middle of the night and dragged out of the tent kicking and screaming, not by a rabid grizzly, but by my Dad who was so excited about seeing the Northern Lights that he wanted us to see it too. He took some photos but they looked like pictures of a vapour trail taken on a cloudy day, in black and white.

After Watson Lake we headed south along Highway 37 which was partly unpaved. We found some beautiful, peaceful wilderness camps next to lakes on this route but one night we stayed on an expensive campsite which was infested with wasps. As we set up the tent we could hear a very loud humming drone coming from the forest nearby but it was only when we began to cook that they descended upon us, buzzing around our heads and landing on our stuff. In the end the three of us had to crowd into the ladies restrooms and cook on the floor in there just to get away from them. Fortunately and not surprisingly we were the only people there.

We made a detour to the town of Stewart then continued for twenty miles up a steep dusty track to see the Salmon Glacier, the largest in North America that can be viewed from a road. It looked like a huge white serpent, the crevasses and seracs like icy scales on its frozen back. We only had two hours to cycle down the twenty miles of dirt track before it went dark so it was a bit of a white knuckle ride.

Just a few miles on from Stewart is the tiny village of Hyder. To get here you actually have to cross the Canada/USA border into Alaska. The road comes to a dead end after that though so I don't think anyone bothered to check our passports. Our main reason for coming here was to visit the Fish Creek bear observatory where we had great views of the bears chasing the salmon across the river and eating them on the banks. I got a great video of two juvenile grizzly brother bears standing on their hind legs and wrestling.

After Stewart we joined the Totem Pole Trail. We stayed near the village of Gitanow, home of the Gitxsan people. There were about fifty totem poles here. They were very tall and some of them looked old with no paint left on the wood. One of them had a big hole all the way through it which was used as a doorway to the longhouse when the village was at war.

Totem poles have many purposes. Some are raised to mark a significant event. Many tell a legend or story. The traditional carvings and artwork of the indigenous people here often include animal designs such as eagle, bear, frog, wolf and raven. Each person belongs to an animal clan. Living in harmony with nature and respecting our fellow creatures has always played an important part in their lives.

We stopped at Morrice Canyon to watch the Wetsu'weten people catching salmon with nets on long poles as they jumped up the waterfall. The people have caught fish here for hundreds of years using fish baskets and gaffs. We bought a whole fresh salmon for our dinner for six Canadian dollars!

We met some very friendly and interesting people in BC. One day we were cycling up a long steep hill in the afternoon heat when a man stopped his car and handed me a brown paper bag. It contained three huge peaches. They were not just any old peaches. These were grown in the Okenagen, famous for its delicious fruit. I will never forget how good they tasted.

Once when we set up our tent next to the tourist information centre, I'm not sure where, a guy pulled up in a big car and started chatting to us. His name was Cam and his wife was called Jacqueline. After a while he asked me if I would like to come and have a sleepover.

'That depends if you have any girls for me to play with' I said.

'Will these do?' Cam pointed to the back seat of his car where Rhianna, aged twelve, Lindsay, aged ten, Sarah, aged eight and Erin, aged four were sitting smiling at me. We cycled to their house and stayed for a night then I stayed and hung out with the girls for a day while Mum and Dad cycled on ahead to the next town where the Malkinson family drove with me to meet them. I had so much fun.

Highway 16 which runs from one side of BC to the other was scary and dangerous. The traffic was heavy and fast. The trucks are twice as long as the ones in Britain with two trailers. When they passed the draught from them sucked and blew us all over the road. Once Mum ended up in a ditch. The worst were the ones carrying wood from the saw mills to the pulp mills in Prince George.

We took a hike along the Ancient Forest boardwalk trail through an inland temperate rainforest to see the gigantic cedar trees, some of which are two thousand years old. We had almost reached the car park when we heard crashing in the trees. There was a black bear sow on the trail just ahead of us.
She was huffing and shaking her head and we got the feeling she wasn't very pleased. Then we saw the reason why. She had sent her two small cubs to the top of a big old cedar tree. It was amazing to watch them climb. They didn't need to use the branches. They just clung to the bark with their sharp claws and ran up the trunk while their Mum stood at the foot of the tree to guard them. Although our bikes were in view we opted to back off slowly and return to the car park the way that we had come.

Mum had to have a tooth taken out in Vanderhoof. The hole started bleeding every time we cycled up a hill.

Riding over the Rocky Mountains

The skies were clear when we passed Mount Robson in the Rocky Mountains. At 3954 metres it is Canada's highest mountain. After this the road between Jasper and Banff, known as the Icefield Parkway is thought by many to be the most beautiful road in the world because of the dramatic peaks and bright turquoise lakes which get their colour from the silt washed down from the glaciers.

We had to climb two passes which were over two thousand metres high. On the way up one of them Mum suddenly keeled over sideways and fell onto the road. It was because her shoelaces had come undone and got caught in the chain.

It was snowing when we arrived at the top of the Sunwapta Pass. We sat in the Icefields centre, sharing a small and very expensive bowl of chips and watched the snow coaches with their huge wheels driving tourists onto the Athabasca Glacier.

We hiked up Wilcox Pass to the alpine meadows where we got very close to a group of bighorn sheep. They looked quite fierce with their huge curly horns but they ignored us and carried on chewing their grass. Our friend Kevin from Calgary, who we had met near Whitehorse, had kindly offered to keep a box of books that we didn't need till later, and he came out with his family to bring out the box and hike with us.

I enjoyed camping on the Parkway because there were cooking shelters where everyone gathered together and talked about their travels. It made a refreshing change from listening to Mum and Dad's conversations which always seemed to be about money (how much over budget we were), maps and distances (how many days behind schedule we were), the new digital camera (it was rubbish) and who's fault things were. (Dad's).

Our friends Michelle and Ike drove over from Red Deer to meet us. We had first met them on the Dempster Highway in their RV on their way up to Fort McPherson where they were helping to build a church. They passed us again on the Stewart Cassiar Highway on their way back, made us a delicious salmon barbecue and told us to phone them when we arrived at Banff. They paid for two nights in a lovely hotel and took us out for steaks in a fancy restaurant in town.

When we were in Banff we met a man who had just cycled all the way across Canada on his own. As he pedalled he made electricity which he stored in a battery attached to his bike. By the end of his journey he had made enough electricity to power the torch for the start of the Winter Olympic Games which was to be held in Vancouver that year. His project was to raise awareness of the potential of human powered electricity which could enable the twelve billion people worldwide without access to the grid to make their own eco friendly power by pedalling.

Mum was more impressed by the fact that he had lost two stone in three months. She hadn't lost any weight so far. In fact she thought if anything, cycling was making her bottom bigger. I think that might have had something to do with all the giant cinnamon rolls she had been eating.

At night we went to the Banff hot springs. They are at the top of Sulphur Mountain and are the highest and hottest public hot springs in the Rockies. The water was 39 degrees but the air was cool and we could see the stars and the lights of the town through the steam.

We had booked out of the hotel by then so had to look for a place to camp in the dark. Eventually we found some park land on the outskirts of town. It was only the next morning that we noticed the 'No Camping. Fine $500' sign. A lady called Susan was walking her dog, Ladybug around the Marsh Loop trail. She let me take the lead for a while which was fine until Ladybug decided to chase a squirrel up a tree, dragging me with her right into the path of a rather grumpy looking elk. Susan has a son, Aaron just a year older than me so after school she took me to meet him and we all went back to the house, ate homemade pizza and watched Cliffhanger. Susan put my bear video onto YouTube where it can still be found under the name 'Grizzly brothers wrestling'.

The fall colours in Kananaskis, south of Banff were spectacular like splashes of bright yellow paint splattered over the mountain sides. After a while we joined the Cowboy Route where we passed cattle ranches full of cows and horses and fields full of hay bails. On one road there was a hat on the top of every fence post for several miles.

We camped on the edge of a field one night. We were woken at first light by mooing and crunching and looked out of the tent to see that we were in the middle of a big herd of cows. Some of them were sitting down. Fortunately none of them had chosen to sit down on our tent which was a similar colour to the pasture land which they were grazing.

After three months we had cycled three thousand miles passing through the four Canadian provinces of the North West Territories, Yukon, British Columbia and Alberta. We crossed the Canada/ USA border at the top of another high pass called Chief Mountain, the Gateway to Montana.

CHAPTER 4

THE UNITED STATES

Cycling through Snowdrifts

Although Glacier National Park was pretty we didn't see any glaciers there. When I asked the park warden she said that the glaciers had receded in recent years and there were only a few small ones remaining. She thought it might be a result of global warming. It was 90 degrees here even though it was late September. One day it was so hot that we had to climb over a fence into a field where there was a big mechanical irrigation system watering the crops, and stand underneath the sprinklers because Mum was afraid that I might be suffering from heat stroke. Little did we know how different the weather would turn out to be just one week later!

On the Montana plains it was flat and windy and there was nothing but straight roads and brown grass stretching on for miles. Big casinos with flashing neon signs lit up the streets of every small town.

Before the arrival of the Europeans this area was home to thousands of buffalo. At the Museum of the Plains Indians we learned about the Blackfeet Tribes who lived in tipis, painted with colourful patterns and pictures of animals and

hunters. They moved around from place to place following the buffalo herds.

When an animal was killed the Indian hunters used every part of the body for food, shelter, tools and beautifully decorative clothing and moccasin shoes. They only killed enough beasts to provide them with what they needed so the population was sustained. When the white man arrived in America, they hunted them in their thousands until, within a few years, the buffalo was almost extinct.

Many dinosaur remains have been found in Montana. In one of the dinosaur museums that we visited there was a life size model of a Seismosaurus, one of the largest of the dinosaurs. It was 150 feet long and 45 ft tall! The Seismosaurus weighed over 50 tons. Its name means ground shaking lizard. We climbed up a hill called Egg Mountain where more dinosaur eggs, baby skeletons and dinosaur embryos have been discovered than anywhere else in the western hemisphere. A huge collection of skeletons of adult Maiasaura dinosaurs were also unearthed, part of a huge herd which palaeontologists believe must have died in a catastrophic event such as an earthquake or hurricane.

Judging by the wind we were experiencing that day, my guess would be that it was a hurricane that knocked them down and was still screaming across the plains trying to do the same to us!

On our journey there were several places where we encountered winds which were so strong that it became impossible for us to cycle. Montana was the first of these. After leaving the top of Egg Mountain we had to push our bikes downhill for ten miles because every time we tried to cycle we were blown over. I had to help Dad just to hold the bike upright. They were the most violent winds that I had experienced. What was more disturbing was that when we called in at the village store the owner assured us that this was not a particularly breezy day by their standards.

That night we found a small woodland park for shelter. The big trees which were gnarled and old looked as if they had lived through a few storms but by 2am the wind was so bad that even their branches were breaking off so, fearing that we might get crushed, we moved the tent into a barn.

We decided to change our route plan and head back towards the mountains in the hope that the forests there would offer some protection from the winds. At the end of September the temperature dropped drastically and stayed that way for the rest of our time in the United States.

Heavy blizzards made it impossible to cycle when we arrived at Boulder so we took the day off and went to the local hot springs where there was an indoor hot tub, sauna, steam room and a big swimming pool where we could relax in the warm water surrounded by snow. It was a pleasant way to spend Mum's birthday which we finished off with a little party feast in the laundry room of the empty campsite with cake, savoury nibbles and wine, spread out over the top of the tumble drier.

At the village of Whitehall most of the buildings were painted with giant murals of scenes from the Lewis and Clark expedition in 1806 when a party of thirty two pioneers made their way across America from East to West.

We pitched our tent at the campground there but when the temperature dropped to 15 degrees below freezing the owners felt sorry for us and insisted that we sleep in their cosy, heated caravan.

On the way up to Yellowstone we camped in the woods next to Quake Lake and woke up to a foot of snow. While we waited for it to clear I made my first snowman of the year. It was the 1st of October! The next night was so cold that the water in our bottles was frozen even though they were inside the tent.

My feet were beginning to get cold on the bike so while we were staying in West Yellowstone Mum bought me some thick fleece lined snow boots. One of the best things we got for the cold weather was a big pack of heat pads which we put inside our socks and gloves. A heat pack looks like a tea bag and once it has been taken out of its plastic wrapper it heats up and stays hot for about six hours. I found that wearing them made a big difference to my comfort in the frosty weather. With toasty hands and feet the rest of my body felt warmer too.

It was so cold in West Yellowstone and the campsites were so expensive that we treated ourselves to a night in a motel room. It was our first non camping night not paid for by someone else. Mum and Dad decided that I deserved a break before the long climb up to Yellowstone National Park which is around 7000 feet in altitude.

On the way up the hill we stopped to watch bison grazing on the side of the road. A hundred years ago bison or buffalo almost became extinct in America. Now there are over four thousand protected by law here in the Park. They are big and woolly with massive heads. A large male can weigh two thousand pounds. That is twenty times more than I weighed at the time. It's best to give them a wide berth as they have been known to attack tourists on occasions when they came too close.

The whole of Yellowstone Park is actually an enormous active super volcano. The last eruption was 640,000 years ago. As we approached Upper Geyser Basin we saw big clouds of steam rising. The smell of sulphur hung in the air. We walked along a boardwalk trail to Fountain Paint Pot where we saw bright turquoise hot springs, bubbling mud pots, spouting geysers and fumaroles belching like giant smoke machines.

There was a layer of frozen snow on the ground making the boardwalks slippery. Even the geysers and boiling hot springs had a crust of ice around the edges. The Old Faithful Visitor Centre had huge icicles hanging from the eaves of the roof and looked like a scene from a Christmas card even though it was only the first week of October.

Old Faithful is the most famous geyser in the park. It is not the biggest but it is the most regular, erupting just about every ninety minutes, sending a huge jet of superheated steam and spray one hundred and fifty feet high.

Once we had watched it go off at half past five we still had seventeen miles to cycle over two 8000 foot passes to get to the next campground. The one near the visitor centre was already closed for the winter and wild camping is forbidden in the park.

When we got to the top of the first pass the snow was a foot thick on the trees and on the side of the road. It looked like Narnia in The Lion, the Witch and the Wardrobe. I half expected to see a faun peering out from behind the trees or a Snow Queen on a chariot. It was getting dark but we knew that we had to keep going because there was heavy snow forecast in two days and we had been told that the road running south from the park exit would not be cleared again this year. It would simply remain closed for the winter.

We stopped and put the lights on our bikes and put new heat packs inside our socks and gloves. By the time we were almost at the top of the second pass I was feeling very weary. What a relief it was when a kind hearted man named Brett stopped his car and offered us a ride down to the next campsite. He somehow managed to pile all our bikes and gear into the back of his pickup then we all squeezed into the warmth of his heated cab for the remaining few miles. We were very grateful to him for saving us from a cold, exhausting ride on a dark, icy road. He even shared his pizza with me!

Next day the really heavy snow arrived and continued for three full days. Soon it was so deep that our tent and bikes disappeared and turned into white lumps. We were unable to cycle over that time. The temperature at night dropped to 18 degrees C below freezing, which was 28degrees C below the average temperature for this time of year.

Our sleeping bags kept us warm enough but we found

camping tough in these conditions, especially sitting outside in the freezing cold, huddled around the stove to cook and eat our meals.

Fortunately we had just made it to a biker/ backpacker Campground by the Grand Teton Lodge which was very cycle friendly. Because we only had bicycles and a tent we only had to pay five dollars a night for the whole family. Also in the evening, in severe weather like this the lodge owner allowed campers to relax in the warm common room where there was a fire, sofas, books and television. There were board games like Earthopoly (the National Parks version of Monopoly) and even computers so Mum could send e mails home and I could play Dress up Dolls.

In the daytime we went for walks in the deep snow and followed the prints of bison, wolves, deer, elk and bear. One morning a wolf ran across our path holding a rabbit in its steaming mouth, dripping with blood.

This was a very sad time for us because we had just heard that my Grandad, Tom had died. We rang him on his birthday, excited and full of news about Yellowstone Park because Tom had always been passionate about geology. We had sent him a postcard of Old Faithful the week before saying 'From an old geyser to another old geyser on your birthday!' and we wanted to know if he had got it but we never got to speak to him again because he had died just a few days before his seventy second birthday.

Grandad was a big part of my life when I was little. He was the most enthusiastic follower of all our adventures. In fact he even came kayaking with us to Alaska and to Thailand, boosting morale when things went wrong with his cheerful outlook and wicked sense of humour. He trekked to Everest Base Camp with us after his second hip replacement and lived in a bothy with our family on the island of Rum so he could look after me after school while Mum and Dad were planting trees.

He stayed with us in Achmore for weeks at a time, fixing the car, gardening, doing DIY and making friends with everyone in the village. I loved sitting in the living room with him watching Time Team and the Grand Prix and having long conversations about people and life.

Grandad was my favourite grown up even though he was often more like a naughty teenager than an adult. He was very untidy and his house was so full of junk that you couldn't see the floor. He refused to throw anything away in case there might be some use for it in the future and he would get very cross when his kids (or their partners) tried to tidy up after him or remove things from the fridge which had green furry growths on them.

Mum and Dad almost decided not to go abroad when they knew that Grandad had cancer but he insisted that they went. He told us that the last thing he wanted was us moping around being miserable while he was ill and that it would benefit him far more if we went away and cheered him up by sending photos or phoning him with stories about our travels. His last words to us were 'Go on kiddies, bugger off and have an adventure!'

His plan was to come out and meet us when we got to Mexico and kayak with us in Baja on the Sea of Cortez. This would give him the incentive to fight his illness and try to get better. When Dad had last called him he had just renewed his passport and had been looking at flights to San Diego for December.

Sadly that never happened and we were heartbroken but we were determined now that we would finish the trip for him. When things got tough and we were tempted to give up and go home, thinking about Tom gave us the strength to carry on. There were many times when it felt like he was with us trying to encourage us like the time when we were in Mexico. Mum and Dad had just worked out that we didn't have enough money to live on for the time it would take to finish the journey, when Dylan, Sean's brother told him on

Skype that Tom had been awarded compensation for his asbestosis caused when he was ship building and his three children would each receive £7000 which was enough for us to keep going for another year.

I never realised how much I would miss my Grandad even now when I'm seven years older.

Eventually the blizzards died down and the snow began to melt. One morning the clouds lifted revealing the serrated ridges of the Grand Teton mountain range dazzling with fresh snow. We cycled south through the famous resort of Jackson Hole and the town of Afton where the largest antler bridge in the USA, made from more than three thousand antlers, forms an archway over the two lane highway. A family of Mormons with ten children gave us a room for the night and dinner. Next morning a lady from the local newspaper came to take our photographs.

Halloween Celebrations in the Desert

The roads around the outskirts of Salt Lake City were busy, fast and dangerous. Although most of the main roads in the US have a shoulder, many of them have a rumble strip running down the centre. This is a bumpy line which is there to warn drivers that they are too close to the edge of the road. The roads are so long and straight in the States that it is easy to lose concentration or even fall asleep. We had to try and keep on the thin bit of tarmac either side of the rumble strip. If we accidentally strayed or got blown onto it when travelling at speed we were likely to get thrown off our bikes.

There wasn't much danger of me falling asleep. Dad and I were connected by the chain so our feet both went round at the same time. I had to pedal at the same speed as him and put in just as much effort especially when we had a hill to climb. He called me the turbo power!

In Evanston we left our clothes in the tumble drier on the COLD setting at the Laundromat while we went to set up camp in the city park. When we returned to pick up our washing all our thermal underwear had melted and turned into twisted pieces of plastic.

We quite often used city parks as a place to camp and we tried to do our bit by picking up rubbish and binning it while we were there.

After Salt Lake the scenery started to look more like desert with small cacti, lizards and expanses of red sand. Moab is famous for its red rock and National Parks such as Canyonlands and Arches where the wind and weather has sculpted the sandstone into amazing shapes.

It was extremely cold when we arrived at Moab especially at night when the temperature dropped to well below freezing but the campsite that we stayed on had a heated outdoor swimming pool and wonderfully warm restrooms. Mum and I spent ages in the restrooms having showers, brushing our hair, reading and playing cards. We were the only campers there.

It was nearly Halloween which has always been my favourite time of year at home. I love carving pumpkins and going round all the houses in fancy dress with my friends. People in our village really go to town with the spooky decorations. We usually have a smoke machine and a green slime chocolate fountain to dip grape marshmallow eyeballs and a candy floss maker for making green candy floss. For the first time on the journey I was feeling a little bit homesick.

Mum was determined to find somebody my age to do 'Trick or Treat' with or 'Guising' as we call it in Scotland. She and Dad spent two days lurking in shops trying to spot a suitable 'friend' for me. It's a wonder they never got arrested. Fortunately when I met Corrina in a thrift store her parents were very understanding when Mum asked if we could join them for Halloween. They invited us for dinner and a sleepover and we soon became good friends.

On the night of the 31st we decorated our bikes. We

carved out three pumpkins and put them in the back of our trailer with branches and leaves and a spooky helium balloon. I was dressed as a witchy vampire. Mum and Dad wore scary pumpkin masks with their black hooded fleece tops. They cycled round on the tandem pretending to be the Black Riders. During the day I made pumpkin masks for Otter and Floppy.

Halloween is BIG in America. People start preparing for it weeks in advance. I could not believe the size of some of the pumpkins for sale. We all met at the school just after dark. Corrina was a bat. Her Mum and little sister, Tyler, were pirates. The streets of Moab were amazing. It was like a Halloween theme park! People had decorated buildings and gardens like haunted houses or the ghost train at a funfair. There were carriages full of skeletons, ghosts floating from the trees, giant illuminated spiders and gardens were lit up with hundreds of grimacing pumpkin faces. The streets were full of people in all kinds of fancy dress although people kept coming up to my parents and complaining that their Black Riders disguise was frightening the children.

On the day after Halloween the town of Moab hosts the annual Pumpkin Chuckin' Festival where teams in costume compete to try to break the record distance for throwing a pumpkin. Each team uses a home made contraption called a trebuchet. We saw all kinds of different structures, some as tall as houses with weights on one end and catapult slings on the other, some which looked more like cannons. By the end of the morning the nearby fields were splattered with squashed pumpkins. Pumpkin Chuckin' competitions take place all over the country but the world record winning throw of one whole mile took place in Moab that year.

There was also a bike jumping competition where people on mountain bikes rode off the top of a bus, down a ramp and performed stunts off the top of two piles of sand. Some of the competitors went really high and did whole somersaults on their bikes.

My stash of Halloween treats made a good trail mix for our detour into Arches National Park. The whole area used to be underneath the sea. There are hundreds of sandstone archways created by the weathering action of wind and frost. Many can be seen from the road or by taking a short hike on one of the many trails. Our favourite was called Delicate Arch.

In addition to impressive rock formations we saw horse petroglyphs carved by the Ute Indians who lived there three hundred years ago. Along the Potash road there were more petroglyphs made by the Fremont Indians over two thousand years ago showing hunters chasing bighorn sheep. Nearby we could see the footprints of a real dinosaur.

During our stay in Moab we hired a car and drove to Mesa Verde in Colorado. This is where the Ancestral Puebloans, once known as the Anasazi, meaning ancient ones, built their homes in the sides of giant cliffs around eight hundred years ago. The remains can still be seen today.

The National Parks in America each have their own Junior Ranger programme for children, which was great for my home education project. We were given a workbook to fill in and a list of activities to carry out, which were designed to help us learn about the history and geography of our surroundings as we explored the park. Once I had completed the programme I was given my Junior Ranger Badge. So far I have badges for Glacier Bay, Arches, Mesa Verde and Grand Canyon Parks.

As part of the programme we had to go on a guided walk led by a Park Ranger, in this case a tour of the ancient dwellings of Cliff Palace, to learn a little bit about how the people here used to live. We had to scramble down many ladders and steep stone steps as we made our way along the narrow rock ledges. The ranger talked a lot and was very bossy. She told mum off for taking photographs while she was talking and after that nobody dared to take any.

We enjoyed Spruce Tree House more because we were allowed to wander around on our own and see how the inhabitants built walls of sandstone bricks and clay using the natural overhangs and alcoves in the cliffs. I climbed down a ladder through a hole into a round chamber with a fire pit, which was called a Kiva. The Kiva was an important room, used for gatherings, ceremonies and storytelling. Women went there to give birth to their babies. We could still see the black soot from the fires clinging to the ceilings of the overhanging rocks.

We stayed for ten days in Moab. I was sad to have to leave Corrina and her family but we arranged to meet up and cycle together in a few weeks time.

Before we left, a lady called Jeannine, who had a garden full of plastic pink flamingos, interviewed us for an article in the Moab Times Independent.

On our way out of Moab another teddy bear joined our team. He was a toy dog. We found him lying on the side of the road all squashed and torn. Cars had driven over him and he had lost his eyes. Dad helped me mend him and Mum bought some new eyes for him. I called him Patchit.

We cycled through Monument Valley, the home of the Navajo people. There were stalls by the side of the road selling dream catchers and beautiful jewellery. I bought a bracelet made of silver and pieces of turquoise mined in Arizona. It had a little Kokopelli symbol on it. The Kokopelli symbol is found in much of the art work around here. He is a fertility god who plays the flute.

We followed a narrow road to the Betatakin Ruin, part of the Navajo National Monument. This is another cliff dwelling of the Ancestral Puebloans. The Hopi people who live here now have descended from them. Our ranger, Patrick, who was from the Sun clan, took us on a long hike into a deep steep sided canyon where we saw the ruins beneath an enormous cave roof.

While we were camping at Betatakin it snowed heavily and we were stranded for a few days. We followed trails through the juniper and pinyon forest and learned about how the different plants have been used for food, medicine and all sorts of other things. The pinyon tree is where pine nut kernels come from. The forest floor was covered with them. We tried picking them ourselves and breaking them out of their shells but it was very fiddly and took us ages to shell one nut. It was much easier to buy a bagful of ready peeled ones from one of the many stalls along the sides of the road.

Our cycle route to the rim of the Grand Canyon took us from 4000feet to 7500 feet in a few hours, the equivalent of cycling up a Munro. The view from the top was worth it though even if Mum made Dad and me stand precariously close to the edge holding the tandem (and trying to look natural) so she could get a good record shot.

The Grand Canyon, which is over a mile deep, has been carved by the River Colorado, exposing the many layers of rock formed over millions of years. At sunset, when we hiked the trail below the rim, the colours of the different types of rock looked especially beautiful in the evening light.

Camping by the roadside near Sedona we were woken several times by a family of skunks outside the tent, climbing into our panniers and raiding the bread bag. In the end Dad had to go outside and bring all the bags inside. I got a glimpse of them in the moonlight. They were very cute with pointy faces and big fluffy tails but they smelt worse than my parents.

Talking of which, my Mum was sitting outside a supermarket in Flagstaff. She had her head in her hands and was looking glum because we had just cycled downhill for two miles before realising that we had taken a wrong turning and were going to have to cycle back up that steep hill to the last junction. A man walked over to her, handed her two dollar notes and said 'God bless you this Thanksgiving!' It

was about time the three of us got a hotel room and spruced ourselves up a bit.

There was no chance of that happening in Sedona. The hotels were all very expensive and even the campsites only took RVs. There was no place in this up market tourist resort for a family of raggedy vagabonds in a tent. Fortunately, as we stood outside the tourist office wondering where to go next, a kindly lady took pity on us and gave us a room in her house for the night. We took showers, washed and dried our grubby clothes and left the next day, full of home made tamales.

We were joined in Sedona by Mickey and Corrina. They cycled with us for three days while Kurt and Mickey went on ahead in the RV, found camping, cooked dinner and got a fire going. We all enjoyed having a support vehicle with us for a change, especially as we could put all our heavy gear from the trailers inside it.

On Thanksgiving night we camped out in the woods surrounded by huge ponderosa pine trees. We had a big feast around a big fire knowing that, for once, we didn't have to worry about it as both Mickey and Kurt are professional fire fighters.

Corrina and I found a fairy tree. We wrote a letter to the fairies and left a plate of food for them. Next morning the food and the letter had disappeared and in their place were two dream catchers and a wand made from things found on the forest floor. I hate to sound cynical but one of the dream catchers did look suspiciously like something my Mum might have made (and not very much like a dream catcher).

As we entered the Arizona desert Dad and I had a bet to see who could spot the first Saguaro cactus. They are the ones you see in cartoons of the desert. They are as big as trees and spiky with huge arms on each side which point upwards. I won the $20. We were so excited to spot our first one that we stopped for a family photo next to it. Around the corner there were literally hundreds of them growing all the way up the surrounding hillsides. We also saw barrel cacti as tall as me with their bright yellow flower tops, organ pipe cacti, giant prickly pear and cholla cacti which spit their prickles at you if you get too close.

Up until now our special Marathon Plus tyres with their strong Kevlar liners had prevented us from getting any flat tyres at all in over five thousand miles but here in southern Arizona where the roads were covered in spikes and thorns it was hardly surprising that there was the occasional puncture to mend or inner tube to replace, especially on the trailers.

In Tuscon we stayed at a flat belonging to our friends, Pat and Teri. It was wonderful to have a real bed to sleep in and a kitchen to cook in and to get a break from the long dark freezing nights in the tent.

On my ninth birthday Pat took us out to a very posh restaurant where I had lobster. My Grandma, who lives in Texas, flew over to stay with us. For Christmas she bought us all a netbook, a small laptop which revolutionised our travelling lives.

My parents are dinosaurs. At the start of this trip they did not have a laptop or a mobile phone. During the first five months of our ride through Canada and Alaska we wasted hours traipsing up and down streets trying to find internet cafes or libraries where Mum could send her monthly newsletter home and pick up messages from her friends and family.

Unlike nearly all the other long distance cyclists that we met, we didn't have a blog or any knowledge of social networks such as Facebook. Mum simply couldn't understand why it was so difficult to find computers available for public use. 'Wifi', on the other hand, or even 'Free Wifi' was advertised everywhere – in campsites, cafes and shops.

'What is this Wiffy that you see everywhere?' she kept asking. Eventually the penny dropped. If we had our own laptop we could use it to get the internet wherever there was Wifi. It didn't even need to be plugged in! Even better news was that you could buy little ones called Netbooks which weigh less than a kilogram and fit easily inside a pannier. Mum was much happier once she had made this discovery. Not only could she access her emails more easily, she could also back up and look at her photos and use SKYPE to phone home.

A prime example of me being told to stand next to a dangerous precipice and 'look natural'.

CHAPTER 5

MEXICO

In at the Deep End

My parents were apprehensive about Mexico. We had never been to Latin America and weren't sure what to expect. Where would we stay at night? What would we eat? Would there be stores to buy food like there were in America? Would we be able to find fuel for the Trangia stove and how would we manage with speaking in a different language?

Mum had done a beginners course in Spanish before we left so she had learned a few basic sentences. Dad and I didn't know any Spanish at all.

People kept telling us how dangerous Mexico was, especially near the borders. At the time there had been a lot of fighting between the different drug cartels and people had been shot dead.

Pat, who was on his way down to Alamos, in the Mexican state of Sonora, insisted on driving us across the border and down to the first big town, fifty miles along the road. As we passed the border station into Mexico, there were groups of fierce looking guards holding large guns but they smiled at me and we didn't have to duck any bullets.

Pat accompanied us to Immigration to apply for our

tourist visas, drove us to Santa Ana where he paid for a hotel room and wished us good luck as he drove away. Concerned for our welfare on the busy and dangerous Highway 15, he had tried to persuade us to stay in the car all the way to Alamos, but we decided to cycle there anyway. It would take us about two weeks and we would get there in time to spend Christmas with them. Until then we were on our own.

Mum had thought that, because Mexico was next to the US, that most people would speak English, especially near the border and we would be able to break ourselves in gently as we learned to get by in another language. They hoped that Mexico would be the country where we could practise our Spanish before cycling into Central America for real.

They were wrong! As soon as we crossed the border hardly anybody we met spoke English. We were in at the deep end and had to learn fast! It wasn't long before I could say basic things like *Hola* (Hello), *Como Estas?* (How are you?), *Adios* (Goodbye), *Gracias* (Thank you), *Quiero* (I would like) and *Donde Es?* (Where is?)

Mum knew how to say quite a lot of things but couldn't understand what people were saying to her. According to her the Mexicans didn't speak Spanish properly like she did. Their Spanish was 'far too fast and the words all jumbled together!'

One of the first and most important sentences we had to learn was '*Podemos a camper aqui por favor?*' which means 'Can we camp here please?' There were no campsites in this part of Mexico and hotel rooms here were still too expensive for our budget. People had warned us not to camp on the side of the road in the middle of nowhere either because it might be dangerous. We were advised to ask people if we could camp in their garden or on their land.

During the first few weeks we found ourselves camping in some strange places including a scrap yard, a cemetery, a car wash and a school. Sometimes, if we stopped for a snack at

a *Ristorante*, the owners allowed us to pitch our tent in their grounds.

Because our first five hundred miles was on a busy motorway our best bet was usually the PEMEX petrol stations that we came across every fifty miles or so. They had toilets and running water and sometimes a little shop. We found that if we approached the armed guards who stood outside every petrol station and asked if we could pitch our tent nearby they nearly always said '*Si!*'

It wasn't long before Mum and Dad were sending me over to do the asking. Being little and cute, unlike them, usually guaranteed positive results so, when it came to finding places to stay, they exploited my cuteness shamelessly.

We soon got used to sleeping through the noise of engines roaring, hydraulic brakes hissing and the ground rumbling beneath our tent as the big trucks thundered by throughout the night.

Driving through Hermosillo, our first major city was quite daunting. It has a population of over one million and we were there at rush hour. There were about six lanes of very dense traffic. Cars brushed against us as they passed, nearly pushing us over. There seemed to be no road rules, just a lot of loud beeping.

I have never seen so many bodies squeeze into the back of one vehicle as I did in Mexico. Often we saw about twenty people clinging to the back of a pick up, all piled up on top of one another along with furniture, mattresses, bikes and goodness knows what else.

The light was beginning to fade when Mum saw what she thought might be a cheap motel room. The sign said '*Habitaciones 200 Pesos*' which was the same as round about fifteen dollars and affordable for us. Mum knocked at the door and asked the lady if she had room for three people. She took one look at us, shook her head and laughed. The 200 Pesos was for four hours, not the whole night. In other words

these motel rooms were intended for couples to go and have a good time in, not for tired dirty cycling families to rest their weary legs!

We continued to search, hoping to find something more suitable as darkness fell, but, judging by all the neon hearts and cupid signs lighting up the walls of every building, there were a great deal more loving couples looking for somewhere to have fun, than tired, dirty cycling families in this part of Mexico.

That was the night that we ended up pitching our tents next to a scrap yard on the outskirts of Hermosillo.

Navigating our way through large towns almost always turned out to be a traumatic experience for our family, particularly in Central and South America. According to Mum there were practically no road signs, those that existed were very misleading and the maps we carried bore very little resemblance to whichever town we were trying to find our way around.

Usually we ended up having to ask for help. This was stressful, especially to begin with. Dad knew very little Spanish so, once we had begun our conversation with '*Para ir a* wherever?' he had no idea what the reply to the question actually meant.

Mum, on the other hand, having studied the chapter 'Finding your way around' in her 'Spanish for Beginners' book, knew quite a bit more. Unfortunately she is incapable of following or remembering travel directions in any language, even English.

However between them they devised a system of getting where they wanted to go. We would cycle up to somebody on the street and ask how to get to a certain place. The person would point and reel off a long list of instructions. We would then smile and nod gratefully and convincingly, before heading in the direction that they had first pointed. We would keep going until we arrived at the next junction or place where a choice needed to be made. Then we would find another person and repeat the whole procedure.

Fortunately in the cities of Central and South America there never seemed to be a shortage of pedestrians to help us. However, the method was long winded, time consuming and not completely foolproof. There was more than one occasion where we were sent around in a big circle only to find ourselves back where we started!

Bimbo, La La and Horny Puffs

We tried out various different types of Mexican food from stands on the side of the road. 'Tacos' are tortilla wraps filled with *frijoles* (beans), *pollo* (chicken), *carne asada* (roast meat) or pescado (fish). They usually come with guacamole and salsa.
Because Dad was vegetarian he usually got *quesadillas* (cheese tacos).

We were keen to sample the local cuisine but, with even street food costing too much to feed all three of us every day, most mealtimes found us sitting cross legged on the pavement outside *abarotes* (grocery stores) or petrol station shops, huddled around a giant pot of strawberry yoghourt (La La!), piling plastic cheese singles and processed ham onto white sliced bread (Bimbo) which contained so many preservatives that it would last in our panniers for over a fortnight without going stale, and stuffing our faces with Hornitos, cheesy puffs which came in a monster sized packet and had flavourings and colouring which turned our tongues, fingers and clothes bright orange.

To make up our 'Five a day' our staple diet of La La, Bimbo, Hornitos (or Horny Puffs as we called them) and other such delicacies was washed down with a large carton of *Durazno* (peach juice)

Whenever we stopped to eat we were surrounded by a motley crew of stray dogs of many different shapes and sizes. We shared our ham sandwiches with them and they stood guard outside our tent at night. Often packs of dogs chased after our bikes, yapping, barking and occasionally growling. We had to take care to avoid getting bitten because of the danger of catching rabies so at first we carried water pistols in our pockets but no dog ever tried to bite us. Most of them just wanted to be friends.

Sometimes they weren't interested in our food. They just liked our company. There was one little cream Labrador with one pointy ear and one droopy ear which would not stop following us. We bought him a tin of meat but he wasn't interested. He just wanted to be our dog and he trotted along with us next to our bikes to the outskirts of the town. We were worried that he might get hit by a car so Dad took him back to the place we had first seen him and asked a shopkeeper to hang onto him for a while so we could make an escape. Despite all this he still managed to catch up with us four miles down the road. We found situations like this upsetting. It was difficult not to get attached to them. I often wished that we could take them with us or at least find a nice home for them.

When you are on a long cycling journey you get to see the worst of places as well as all the wonderful tourist attractions. Sometimes, on the outskirts of town the piles of rubbish were so thick that it was difficult to know whether we were cycling through a landfill site or not. We passed a lot of road kill – cats, snakes, cows and mainly dogs. We could smell the stench as we approached and tried to hold our breath for as long as it took us to cycle past. The other warning of a recent road kill was the clusters of giant vultures perched on the branches of roadside trees, swooping down and dodging the traffic to peck at the rotting carcasses.

In many ways we found travelling through Mexico quite

tough. Never knowing if we would be able to find a safe place for the night was particularly stressful. Looking back with nostalgia however, we all agree that this country holds some of our favourite memories.

Mum believes that travelling is a good way of restoring faith in human nature because of her experiences of the kindness of strangers especially when abroad. Although we had been warned many times that Mexico was dangerous, we encountered some of the kindest, most generous people we could hope to meet. Every day people who had never seen us before went out of their way to help us in any way they could (Especially when they saw me!).

Not many days after we had crossed the border a big rusty old car pulled up into the lay-bye we were cycling past. A huge, fierce looking guy with a bushy moustache and scary tattoos all over his muscly arms yelled to us and waved us over to his car. Nervously we wheeled our bikes towards him.

'I thought we weren't supposed to approach parked cars' Mum muttered.

'I wouldn't want to offend him' whispered Dad. The man proceeded to open his boot and lift out a large case. It contained a table and several folding chairs. He gestured to us to sit down while he pulled out two cool boxes and plastic bags containing cerviche (a raw seafood dish), salad, bread and cakes. He called to the people in the car and a lady with three little girls climbed out.

'*Buen Provecho*!' he ordered us which means 'Enjoy your meal' From what Mum could understand, the family, who were from Hermosillo, were driving down to the Sea of Cortez for a day on the beach but when they saw us they decided to have their picnic with us on the side of the motorway instead.

Another night when we were about to set up camp behind a petrol station a man came over and said that it wasn't safe to stay there. He told us to go with him and drove his car very slowly so we could follow him down a muddy track, through a wood and across four fields. We wondered where he was taking us. Eventually he stopped next to a small ramshackle barn. Inside was a small room with a bed, a table, a chair, a sink in the corner and several small statues of Jesus and the Virgin Mary. He told us that it was his brother's house and he was away so we could stay there for the night. He wished us 'Buenas Noches' telling us that he was going back to his own house in the village but when Mum looked out in the middle of the night she saw him sleeping in a hammock outside so I think that he had given up his own little home for us so we would be safe.

Toilet Trolls and the Proud Poo

Mum always says that one of the best things about this type of travel is how the simple luxuries that we take for granted at home become really special treats when you have been deprived of them for a while; A hot shower when you are cold and filthy, a cheap hotel room with a bed when you've been camping on the side of the road for weeks, a cooked meal when you're starving hungry or the chance to watch a TV programme in English. All the little things which you wouldn't think twice about at home become something that you value and look forward to. When we were living this lifestyle it seemed to take so much less to make us happy.

Talking of learning to appreciate the simple things in life, even getting to use the toilet at the right time seemed like a bonus, especially for us girls. Unlike sea kayaking, where we were usually in the wilderness, on bikes we were rarely out of view of other people. Mum, who needs to pee at least three times a night had to have a bucket with a lid inside the tent. Number twos were even more of a challenge. Public toilets were few and far between so the chances of all of us finding one at the right time were pretty slim. Mum found that sometimes, even if she had been desperate to go for ages, when she finally found somewhere she felt under so much pressure to make the most of it, she was unable to produce anything.

It didn't help that most public toilets were zealously patrolled by the cleaning staff (or toilet trolls as we called them). They lurked outside the door or next to the sink. In order to gain entry you had to give them 2 Pesos in return for a piece of toilet paper. It wasn't that we begrudged them the money. In fact Mum said that she would happily give them ten times that amount if they would just go away for a little while. We found it quite difficult to do what we had gone in there to do when there was somebody hovering impatiently right outside the cubicle with a mop, anxious to clean up after us before our bottoms had even made contact with the toilet seat.

For this reason any of us who managed to start the day off having done a nice big poo felt especially smug. It felt like a good omen and whoever was in luck that day boasted to the others about it. It was from this trip that the term 'Proud Poo' originated.

The further South we cycled the warmer it became. After six months of cycling we finally arrived at the sea side. We found a lovely quiet beach near San Carlos where we camped, swam and gathered beautiful shells while dolphins danced and pelicans dive bombed. I was also fortunate enough to be taken on a detailed guided tour of all the paint and DIY shops in San Carlos as part of Mum and Dad's yet uncompleted mission to find a substitute for methylated spirits for their stove.

This part of Mexico is called Sonora. Some of it is desert but the part that we cycled past consisted mainly of ranches and farmlands irrigated by canals. We saw many crops growing such as corn, tomatoes, chilli peppers, beans and chickpeas. Many of the farmers here round up their animals on horseback.

The pitaya dulce cacti, which we saw everywhere, are also known as the organ pipe cacti. They look similar to the saguaro but have numerous long branches pointing upwards like pipes. Sadly much of the cacti forest is dwindling here as they are being chopped down to make room for agriculture.

After two weeks on Highway 15 we left the coast and cycled up into the mountains. Our friends, Pat and Teri, live in Alaska in the summer months and in the winter they live in Alamos where they run La Puerta Roja (The Red Door) Inn. It was the loveliest building I have ever stayed in. The rooms were painted with bright colours and filled with unusual paintings, sculptures and ornaments. On the beds there were beautifully embroidered cushions and patchwork quilts. There were pretty things and funny things from markets and shops in many different parts of the world. There was a courtyard in the middle full of plants and flowers and a purple swimming pool.

Many parts of Central and South America were colonised by the Spanish when they came over to America in the 16th Century. Alamos, a typical colonial town has many grand looking stone buildings, painted white with majestic arches and pillars. The streets are narrow and cobbled and in the centre there is an old cathedral and a plaza (town square) with an outside market where we bought *churros* which were similar to doughnuts, fried in a big metal bin over an open fire.

In Mexico we saw many shrines and big statues of the Virgin Mary. There is a famous legend here about a church near Alamos. The story goes that some miners saw a vision of the Virgin Mary at the very top of a saguaro cactus. They piled up stones so that they could climb up to her but when they got there she faded away like a ghost. When they reached the ground they discovered that, by moving the stones, they had exposed a vein of silver. They followed the vein which happened to be leading them in the same direction as the cactus was pointing and it led them to the main seam of silver. A mine was built and Alamos became a wealthy town. When they built the church there a saguaro cactus grew out of the wall and pointed to the mine. This can still be seen there today.

A Scorpion in my Stocking!

On Christmas Eve we cycled down to Pat and Teri's beach house on the sea of Cortez. It was twenty miles away from the main road along a sandy dirt track which meanders through a giant pitaya cactus forest. After about ten miles the sand became very thick and soon it was pitch dark. Our bikes were heavily loaded with food and presents for Christmas day and we kept skidding in the deep sand and falling off. Potholes filled with water spanned the whole width of the track. There were numerous forks with tracks leading off in different directions and soon we became resigned to the fact that we were lost.

I felt scared so Mum got us all to pretend that we were the three wise men following the star and we sang some Christmas carols. I was glad that we had our French Canadian cycling friend JF with us. We had first met him when we were camping at the Grand Canyon and then we had bumped into him along the road just two days ago.

Eventually we decided that there was no point in trying to find our way in the dark. We found a small clearing to pitch the tents, lit a small fire, drank some of the Christmas cider and ate the chocolate presents. Close to midnight fireworks from nearby houses began to explode and light up the sky.

On Christmas morning, instead of finding a stocking full of presents at the end of my bed I found a scorpion next to my sleeping mat. Very slowly Dad lifted the mat and dropped it outside the tent where the scorpion instantly vanished in the sunlight.

It must have been brought in on our clothes the night before after we had been sitting out by the fire. It was a reminder to us to always check our clothes and shoes before putting them on and not to leave things lying around outside the tent at night. We found out later that a sting from one of these scorpions is often deadly and we had just spent the night sleeping next to one! Around a thousand people in Mexico die each year from scorpion stings. Even if you manage to get medical help in time, unless you have kept the scorpion or have taken a really good photo, it is difficult for the doctors to know which antidote to use, as the venom differs in each type of scorpion.

On Christmas Day Pat came out in his Jeep to find us and drove us the remaining few miles to the beach house. It is on an estuary filled with thousands of birds. There were grey pelicans and flocks of white pelicans with bright yellow bills, herons and big frigate birds with forked tails.

The dolphins there swam close to shore nearly all the time.
We paddled out in the kayaks to explore the mangrove covered islands. The dolphins followed us around, jumping and playing by the side of our kayaks.

In the afternoon I listened to my new MP3 player while the grown ups got drunk. Later on we painted little reindeers silver and gold as we decorated the room for dinner and present swapping.

We were sad to have to leave our friends but it was time to get back on the road before we started to get too comfortable. We had another week on the main road before we joined the Mex 200, which follows the coast of Mexico for another thousand miles. We passed orange and lime orchards and plantations of a spiky plant which looked like Aloe Vera but turned out to be Agave from which the drink tequila is made.

As we got closer to the sea we were surrounded by swamps and lagoons full of big birds with bright pink wings.

Mum thought they were flamingos but apparently the name of these birds is roseate spoonbills and it is believed that their feathers are pink as a result of the large amounts of shrimp in their diet.

I can clearly remember sitting on a concrete slope beneath a road bridge, next to a busy motorway eating *camarones secos* (dried shrimps) that we had bought from one of the many stalls near the Sea of Cortez.

The swamps are also a habitat for crocodiles which can grow to be seven metres long. They usually eat small mammals, birds and fish. Attacks on humans are very rare although they have been spotted on the beaches occasionally.

It was beginning to feel much warmer now. We regularly spotted large, furry orange and black tarantulas attempting to cross the road. A big occasion for us was the day when we crossed into the Tropic of Cancer, 23 degrees north of the equator. In six months we had cycled all the way from the Arctic to the Tropics!

The Top of the Dinner

Once we had joined the Mex 200 our route followed the coast which meant that there were beaches and occasionally caravan parks for us to camp on. We could cool off in the waves although usually the surf was very rough and, after Mum fell off her lilo and nearly got carried out by a riptide, we were cautious about swimming in the sea.

In Aticama we met Dave and Laura and their friend Chip who were travelling around America with their microlights. They invited us to camp with them and took each of us up for rides in the sky.

It was the most incredible feeling when we took off from the beach and soared up to 2000 feet above the jungle and the sea while the sun set although Mum got travel sick and as for

Dad, well for reasons known best to himself and Chip, it took twice as long for him to come back down to earth once he'd landed than it did the rest of us. When Mum had just been dropped off after her hour long turn at flying she marched up to Dad, who was supposed to be looking after me, and demanded to know where I was, to which he replied vaguely 'Oh I thought she was with you!'

Fortunately I had gone for a walk with Laura and was sitting in her caravan drinking matte tea. I had not been taken by a crocodile or fallen out of a microlight in mid flight.

My violin, which was half size, was getting a bit small for me and I wasn't really playing it very often. Laura took Mum and me to the primary school in Aticama so we could present it to the children there. They were really excited. The headmaster gathered everyone into the hall so that he could introduce us and Mum made me play a tune on it before we handed it over which was quite embarrassing.

Mum had assumed that, because the Mex 200 hugs the coast, our route would be reasonably flat. She was wrong. This was easily the hilliest part of our journey so far. The coastal mountains of Mexico go right down to the sea and between each sandy bay the road winds its way up and up to heights of over 2000 metres before descending to the next one.

We passed old men bent over double as they carried large bundles of firewood on their backs. Sometimes old men bent over double with bundles of firewood passed us! Mum who was trying out her Spanish sometimes asked them if we were nearly at the top of the hill. She found out after a few weeks that what she had actually been saying was 'Are we nearly at the top of the dinner yet?' Five years later on and we still always refer to the top of the hill as the top of the dinner.

At around the same time she discovered that she had been asking for eggs incorrectly. Apparently you are supposed to say '*Hay huevos?*' meaning 'Are there Eggs?'

'*Tiene Huevos?*' which is what she had been saying translates as 'Have you got balls?'

We saw many different types of tropical fruit growing by the road such as bananas, papaya, coconuts and a huge lumpy plant called yaka which has lots of little yellow fruit inside. We bought a water melon every day. Costing around two dollars they were incredibly refreshing and always cool inside no matter how hot the day. The only trouble was, we had to attempt to eat the whole fruit in one sitting because, no matter how many different ways we tried of attaching half a melon to our trailer, it invariably fell off and got lost before we arrived at the next place.

On the top of one hill we met an old man who was pushing a trolley full of ice cream. He had pushed it nearly three miles from his home to sell on the next beach. The trolley was not refrigerated and the ice creams were melting in the hot sun. We felt so sorry for him that we bought three ice creams each and nearly made ourselves ill eating them before they turned into a runny mush.

Mum's favourite thing about Mexico was the fact that the workmen on building sites and the side of the road wolf whistled and shouted '*Guapa*' at her. This never happens at home and it gave her ego a boost. I didn't have the heart to burst her bubble by telling her that they did the same to me and Dad as well, even when she was nowhere to be seen. I think they whistled at anyone who had long hair and bare legs. The Mexican women all thought that Dad looked like Jesus. They even gave him cakes!

In Rincon de Guayabitos which means Edge of the Jungle we met our friends Judith, Dennis, Cath and Bob who drive down from Canada every year to spend their winter travelling in Mexico. The beach at Rincon was great fun. It was so busy and colourful. There were big stands piled up high with bright inflatable beach toys. I bought a big green inner tube and Mum and I had hours of fun playing on the waves. There were barrows pushed by bikes selling barbecued fish or shrimps on sticks, sticky cakes or tamales.

Early in the morning we walked down to the beach to buy fresh fish and shrimps from the boats. While the fishermen weighed and filleted their catch, hundreds of pelicans crowded round, vying for the scraps. Pelicans in Mexico are very common like seagulls at home.

We had a few frightening moments on the Mex 200. It is narrow and busy and the people drive like maniacs especially on Sundays. Often drivers overtook us when there were cars coming towards us on the opposite side, leaving us very little space and causing us to wobble and nearly fall. Instead of a verge or shoulder there was nearly always a deep stone ditch on the side of the road which would have been very nasty to get knocked into.

In Punta Perula we pitched our tent on the rooftop of a beach house belonging to our friends, Alan and Dianne. They said it was safer than on the ground because of the scorpions. Dianne had made the most amazing mosaic in the bathroom with an intricate turtle design tiling the entire wall. Next morning we borrowed their kayaks and paddled out to a rocky islet to snorkel. The surge of the swell made it quite scary but we got to see some pretty tropical fish such as angelfish and Moorish idols.

In Melaque we stayed with some Canadian friends we had met along the road. Their names were Nancy and Drew (Yes Really!) Nancy and I took a yoga class on the beach and then practised on the roof. They took us down to La Manzanilla and Boca beaches where, in the lagoons, right next to the trail, we passed huge wild crocodiles basking in the swamps. All that exists to separate the people from the crocodiles is a thin yellow tape and a PELIGROSO (Danger!) sign showing a picture of a big open crocodile mouth. On one of the signs the picture showed a crocodile mouth with a dog running into it. At the end of the trail was a beach where tourists sunbathed and swam less than two hundred metres from the swamp!

After leaving Nancy and Drew's house we spent two days with Jim and Merilee from Vancouver. Merilee took me down to the beach to get my hair braided into dozens of tiny beaded plaits by two local ladies indigenous to the area. Merilee made the most wonderful banana muffins. I enjoyed eating them so much that she promised to come and look out for us on the road in a week and bring us a fresh batch. They had a little trip planned in their RV and told us to leave messages tied to lamp posts to help them find us. After a few days we found a piece of paper stuck to a lamp post with our names written on it. They had looked everywhere and left notes all over the place but that was the only one we found.

We camped at Ixtapilla next to a well known turtle beach. The Olive Ridley turtles come up at high tide to lay their eggs and bury them in the sand at the back of the beach. We walked along the dunes where there were hundreds of old broken turtle eggs which smelled quite strongly. We could also clearly make out the tracks of the turtles which had visited the beach on the previous night.

That evening we sat on the beach at about 10 pm watching the moonlight gleaming on the spray from the huge surf waves. We could not see any turtles. A man called Francisco started chatting to us. He was an expert on turtles and offered us to walk down the beach with us and help us to spot one. As we walked along he pointed out new tracks and then showed us where a turtle was laying her eggs. He told us that she would probably lay around one hundred eggs in a few places. When she had finished we watched her walk slowly back towards the sea. She looked exhausted but she managed to make her way out through the huge breakers and disappear into the ocean.

At certain times of the year in the rainy season the turtles come up the beach to nest in large numbers, a phenomenon which is known as La Arribada. Ixtapilla is one of the only twelve beaches in the world where this happens. A few years ago the number of turtles to arrive at Ixtapilla was diminishing rapidly so the local people took action and turned their beach into a protected reserve. At first they struggled to get support from the government but eventually their efforts paid off and the project has been very successful.

Next morning Mum and I walked back to the same spot to see if we could see any traces of the last night's events and there was another turtle plodding up the beach, its wet shell shining in the sunlight.

The eggs hatch forty five days after they have been laid and the tiny baby turtles have to dig themselves out of the sand and make their way down to the sea before birds or other predators can eat them.

Not many of the hundreds of eggs laid survive to adulthood. To give them a better chance locals have set up Tortuga sanctuaries along the coast. They collect the eggs and bury them in a safe place, enclosed by mesh so that dogs or other animals cannot dig them up and eat them. When the turtles hatch they put them in a pen for a day before carrying them part of the way down the beach where they are released. The people then stay with the turtles, walking next to them on the first stages of their big journey, protecting them from gulls until they have reached the water.

At Playa Azul we joined a group of school children who were helping out with this task. There were about two hundred baby turtles, all raring to go and scrabbling about excitedly in the pen. I picked one up. It was the size of my hand and the shell was still soft. The lady put some in a bucket and we went with her to set them free. Each person was responsible for one turtle. It was amazing how, once they had been placed on the ground, they all instinctively knew which direction to go – with the exception of Mum's turtle that is, which for some reason repeatedly headed off towards the houses. Typical that Mum would pick the only turtle with no sense of direction!

We watched the little newborns disappear into the turbulent water and wished them well on their journey.

Mexico is full of Beetles – cars, not insects. In Acapulco every other car was a VW Beetle. They even used them as taxi cabs. Climbing up the long steep hill out of the city on the hottest day I have ever experienced is something I will never forget. We nearly collapsed from heat exhaustion halfway up despite having spent an hour bathing in the tepid sea water of Acapulco beach in an effort to cool off before we began our ascent. Thankfully we found a campground on the outskirts of town with a large cool swimming pool.

After Acapulco the tourist trail peters out. We saw no towns or resorts for seven days and didn't meet a single holiday maker. It felt as if we had travelled back in time. Goats, pigs, hens, roosters and turkeys roamed freely along the road. The meat must be 'happy meat' here. One turkey was even lounging in a hammock! We watched small boys leading donkeys with rope and moustachioed men, wearing sombrero hats, riding frisky horses to herd the cattle.

Dogs lay listlessly on the road. By this time it was so hot that they could no longer be bothered to get up and chase us. Little children with bare feet giggled and shouted 'Gringos!'' at us when we passed. We looked down on wide rivers where crowds of people huddled by the water, washing clothes and hanging them out in long colourful lines to dry in the sun.
We stopped for a coke at stalls where people cooked seafood outside on clay ovens. One day I watched a lady cooking octopus or *pulpa* in a steaming pot over open flames.

Sometimes we saw pairs of oxen with horns and huge humps on their backs pulling carts or traps with big wooden wheels along the road.

We cycled through forests of palm trees for miles. Huge piles of coconuts and signs for *Coco Frio* (cold coconut juice) dotted the sides of the road. One day a man walked up to us and presented us with a coconut. He skilfully chopped off the top with a single swipe of his machete so that we could drink the juice which tasted fizzy and tangy but quite refreshing.

Even the small towns have big *Pastelerias* (cake shops). They are full of very elaborate party cakes as tall as the shop window, often with six or more tiers. Mum and I really wanted to look inside one so on Valentine's Day we got Dad settled in a café with a coffee while we went to buy him a surprise Valentine's Day cake. They had already sold out but we managed to find a nice small blue cake decorated with hearts and roses. It had the words '*Felicidad*!' written on it which we decided must mean Happy Dad but turned out to mean 'Congratulations!' Mum said that he deserved to be congratulated for being her Valentine for twenty years. The cake was almost entirely made from spray icing so when we walked out into the heat of the day it immediately began to melt into a blob. By the time we had crossed the road to the café it was impossible to read what the writing said anyway so we quickly cut it into pieces and shared it with everybody who was sitting near us.

In Pinotepa Nacional in the plaza at night there appeared to be some kind of festival taking place. Groups of men wearing dark suits and sombreros stood in lines facing one another and danced to a spooky fiddle tune played by an old man. They held a bunch of grass in one hand and a rattle in the other. Their faces were hidden behind sinister looking black and white masks. Mum tried to find out what it was all about but her Spanish wasn't good enough to understand what the spectators told us. She took a few pictures but two of the men chased after her waving their rattles fiercely and scared the life out of me after which I begged to go be taken back to the hotel.

Later we googled Festivals in Oaxaca and found out that the dance, which is popular in this area, is called Los Tejerones meaning The Weavers. It usually takes place in February and March during the period of Lent and it makes fun of some of the ridiculous Spanish colonial rules and traditions. No wonder poor Mum had difficulty translating that!

Mountains, Mayans and Markets

After nearly 2000 miles of cycling along the coast, it was time to leave the sea and head inland towards the mountains. First of all we had to cross La Ventosa which means The Very Windy Place. It is in the narrowest part of Mexico and this piece of land between the Pacific Ocean and the Gulf of Mexico is subjected to very strong winds. In one day in every three it is impossible for traffic to drive along the road. Trucks are regularly blown over onto their sides and we had been warned to be very careful.

We passed hundreds of wind turbines but the wind wasn't too bad until we left the coast and began to cycle up our first twenty mile long hill. After this it became so violent that, not only was it impossible to cycle, but we could barely hold onto our handlebars and push without the bikes being ripped from our grasp and hurled across the road.

We stopped next to a sign with the words Pte Curva de los Vientos meaning Curve of the Winds. A traveller in a small campervan stopped to chat with us. His name was Jon and he was from England. After a brief conversation he offered to drive me up to the top of the hill in his van and wait with me while Mum and Dad continued to push the bikes.

It says a lot about their protective parenting instincts that they happily allowed me to be driven away in a foreign country by a complete stranger without knowing anything about him. Fortunately he was a lovely man and we had a great time sitting at the top of the hill laughing our heads off (not at them I hasten to add!) They arrived a few hours later. Six men wielding machetes had jumped out of their van and offered to give them a lift but, as it was impossible to get all the bikes and trailers inside, they helped to push instead.

We had to camp there amongst the twisted trees with their wildly flailing branches. Jon parked his van next to us to give the tent some shelter but each time I woke up the wind was shrieking and Dad was holding onto the sides of the tent.

After that we had to climb over an 8000 foot pass to get to San Cristobal which is a beautiful city high in the mountains of Chiapas filled with lovely old buildings and cathedrals. We stayed there for two days and visited the plazas and markets where the indigenous people from the mountain villages of Chiapas sell their locally grown produce and brightly coloured embroidery and weavings. Many of the people are Mayan. Some women wear long hairy skirts of thick black wool and shawls of purple and blue, their babies slung to their backs.

At the food markets we saw fruit and vegetables piled up in pyramids on top of little buckets on the ground. There were round sacks and baskets containing many different spices, grains, beans and chillies. People stood in the street holding live chickens upside down in their hands. Pigs' heads were laid out on the tables of the covered stalls.

We stayed in a hostel for the first time and met travellers from all over the world. I hardly saw anything of Mum and Dad. My new friends from Italy took me out to the plaza at night and we played Uno, a card game, with the local kids and I learned how to play Devil Sticks.

On the road to Palenque we passed villages where women and children were traditionally dressed with white frilly blouses embroidered with turquoise and pink. Coffee beans were drying out on sheets in front of their houses. Children stood at either side of the road holding a rope up to stop the traffic and prevent us from passing through until we had bought corn on the cob and sugar sticks from them.

Another hazard for cyclists in Chiapas was the *Topes* or ramps found on the road near the villages. Their official purpose is to slow the traffic down but we couldn't help wondering if their secondary purpose was to entertain the locals by catapulting unsuspecting cycle tourists into the nearest bush as they were often unsigned and very difficult to see. Mum was cycling down one hill when she hit a ramp at full speed, sending her head first over the handlebars. Fortunately she managed to break her fall with her feet before landing on the tarmac in a crumpled heap. Two purple ladies clutched their hairy skirts and laughed at her from the side of the road, confirming our theory about *topes* really being booby traps for gringos.

Mum was relieved to see Dad running down the road towards her with an anxious expression on his face. She wasn't so pleased when he continued to run past her and straight over to the bike to check that the derailleur wasn't damaged, leaving her 'bleeding on the ground' as she put it.

The area between San Cristobal and Palenque is well known for its gorges, waterfalls and natural swimming pools. We visited a few of these. The most famous is Agua Azul because of its picturesque cascades and crystal clear turquoise water which we found very refreshing after a gruelling day of ups and downs (and *topes*).

As part of my home education I was doing a project about the Mayans, one of the most advanced of the ancient American cultures dating back to 1500 BC. They built cities in the rainforests of the Yucatan, Guatemala, Belize and Honduras. We explored the temples of Palenque which was on our route. We walked up and down hundreds of stone steps and through dark passageways where we saw tombs and thrones and statues of Gods and kings carved into the rock. The pyramids and other buildings were once painted red with ink made from squashed beetles and we could still see traces of orange on some of the stones.

On the walls there were hieroglyphs carved inside groups of squares. This is the Mayan writing. Each pictograph stands for a word or an idea and can be put together to tell a story. The Mayan languages are still spoken by the indigenous people of this area. Spanish is their second language.

Inside the museum there were statues of Mayan heads. They had sloping foreheads because they fixed boards to their babies' heads while they were still soft which caused them to slope backwards because this was believed to be beautiful. They also dangled objects in front of their faces to make them go cross eyed as this look was fashionable there in those days.

On the road to Bonampak we stayed at a small village where three little Mayan speaking girls followed us around until Dad gave them each a ride on the back of the tandem.

When we arrived at the ruins of Bonampak early in the morning the atmosphere was quite spine chilling. We were the only people there, a mist hung in the air and a large group of howler monkeys was making an eerie groaning noise in the trees. We climbed some steps into a series of chambers where we saw some gruesome painted murals which depicted a royal ceremony, a battle, the taking of slaves, torture and human sacrifice.

The Mayans believed that the Gods needed blood to nourish them. They also contributed their own blood voluntarily by piercing parts of their body. In one of the paintings three ladies in white robes were piercing their tongues. I was very relieved to hear that human sacrifice is no longer practised by the Mayans in this area although chickens sometimes get used to appease the gods instead. Another interesting religious tradition of the modern day Mayans which we heard about was drinking coke to help them burp out evil spirits.

I wasn't the only one in our family working on a project. The topic which Mum was studying was the beers of Mexico and Central America. It seemed to involve a great deal of research (at least three bottles a night) and hardly any writing.

After three months in Mexico it was finally time to leave the country which we had loved at some times and hated at others. It was the country which we found the toughest but now that we look back at our cycle trip with rose tinted glasses it is always Mexico which we feel most nostalgic about. We were sometimes scared and were often out of our comfort zone there but I remember feeling really alive at that time in my life.

CHAPTER 6

CENTRAL AMERICA

Tarantulas and Poo flinging Primates

To get to Guatemala we had to load our bikes onto a narrow motorboat which took us four miles up a river called the Rio Usumacinta to a tiny village called Bethel. The next village of Tres Cruces was over fifty miles away and connected to Bethel by an extremely rough and rubbly dirt track.

We left Bethel at dawn when the sun was still low in the sky. Women walked along the road with big jugs of water resting on their heads. Unlike the USA/Mexico border which was swarming with armed police and where we had had to queue in heavy traffic for hours to fill in the various forms, the immigration office here consisted of a tiny shed with a solitary border guard who stamped our passport and said 'Bienvenidos a Guatemala!' We were the only visitors there. It wasn't long before the temperature rose to over 35 degrees Celsius and there was no shade from the blinding white sun beating down upon us. The water in our bottles was as hot as tea and tasted of plastic. The surface of the road felt like a scree slope at times so our progress was frustratingly slow. It was one of the hardest days of the journey so far. We had never felt so hot or thirsty or sore in our entire lives.

After miles of nothing but dust and heat we saw some buildings and a road sign. Our spirits lifted, convinced that we must be finally approaching our destination then drooped in disappointment and disbelief as the words 'Tres Cruces 30 Km' slowly became clear enough to read.

Mum burst into tears. She had a sunburned mouth and was so saddle sore that she could no longer sit on her seat. It was dark by the time we eventually hit the paved road and wobbled wearily into town after fourteen gruelling hours on the road.

On the way up to the World Heritage Site of Tikal we met the Miller family, Ezrah, Elijah, Gabe and Hannah and their Mum and Dad, Jenny and Tony. They travel around the world all the time. It is their lifestyle. They had already cycled from Britain to Africa together. Gabe swapped with me and rode on the back of the tandem while I had a ride up to Tikal in the car.

The kids were all around my age so it was fun for me to hang out with them at the campsite and tour the Mayan ruins together. They had mosquito nets which also acted as hammocks so at night they could hang them in a tree with their sleeping bags inside and sleep off the ground. They looked like giant chrysalises in their net cocoons.

Tikal is famous for its tall stone temples which soar high above the dense canopy of tropical jungle. I enjoyed the abundance of wildlife which we encountered while walking the trails much of which I had never seen or heard of before. We caught glimpses of parrots and two types of toucan. There were brightly coloured wild turkeys and an enormous black pheasant like bird with a yellow beak known as a great curassow.

Spider monkeys swung from the trees above. We were amused by the sign which warned us that 'You can also see the howler monkey. They are slow and sedentary. They like to defecate on the heads of the people below and scream loudly

to show their presence.' Fortunately no howler monkeys felt the need to poo on my head while we were in the jungle.

Near the ticket office a man with a pet black tarantula the size of a football was allowing tourists to hold it. I said 'No Thank You'

On the campsite groups of coatimundis wandered around between the tents. They look like a cross between a badger and a racoon. They roamed the field in gangs, scratching their fleas. Apparently domesticated coatimundis are affectionate, intelligent and playful and make great pets but it was the first time I had come across one.

Next to the path was a big tree named the Ceiba Tree. This tree represents the Tree of Life to the Mayans with its roots in the underworld, its trunk in the living world and its branches in the heavens.

Another natural feature of great religious significance to the Mayans is the cenote. A cenote is an underground limestone cavern with the roof fallen in. They are often filled with clear spring water and make wonderful swimming pools. We visited a cenote named The Blue Hole shortly after crossing the border into Belize. In addition to being the main source of fresh water for the ancient Mayans, they were associated with the underworld and connected to the goddess Ixchel and the moon. The blessing of cenote water still takes place during full moon ceremonies and before weddings.

Linked to The Blue Hole by an underground tunnel was St Herman's Cave where Mayans lived in around 900 AD. This cave was a place of homage to Chac, the God of rain and Zibalb, the God of the underworld.

Baked Beans in Paradise

Compared to Guatemala Belize seemed quite posh. The grocery stores were full of exciting things like cheddar cheese, custard and Snickers ice cream. Mum was ecstatic when she discovered cans of real Heinz baked beans on display on the shelves.

The road to the coast took us through miles of orange groves. Ripe oranges were strewn along the roads, having fallen from passing trucks and we stopped to snack on the sweet juicy fruit whenever we felt like it.

For a half way expedition treat we had promised ourselves a week of snorkelling on a tropical island. As usual this had to be done on a budget. When we got to the coast of Belize we found a deal where we could take a boat out to Glover's Reef, a tiny atoll in the Caribbean Sea, 50 km off the mainland. Once ashore we would be able to camp on the beach for a week, using the basic toilet facilities provided and cooking our own meals from food brought with us.

I had a wonderful time. I made two friends my own age. Maddy, aged nine, had lived on the island for the whole of her life. Her teacher Alison comes to the island to give her lessons. I was invited to join in and got to go to school on an atoll! The two of us had great fun dressing up in each others clothes and having fashion shows in the tent.

Eden, aged nine was crazy about animals. We collected lizards together and put out food for the giant hermit crabs. We snorkelled through gardens of fan coral and brain coral surrounded by myriads of tropical fish. Once I swam with a southern sting ray. This is a fish which swimmers must avoid touching. They have vicious barbs on their tails which can inflict very painful wounds. Mum and dad rented a sea kayak so they could paddle out to the best snorkelling spots in the lagoon.

One evening we were down at the dock while the crew were cleaning the fish from the day's catch, when about twenty sting rays swam beneath the deck followed by two nurse sharks. A bull shark came in to eat the scraps just a metre below our feet.

The island was covered with palm trees. In the middle was a table for splitting open the coconuts and a grinder for grinding the meat into coconut rice. We were a little bit nervous about camping close to so many big palm trees. Several holiday makers are killed worldwide by falling coconuts. They are heavy and hard and fall from a great height. My Aunty Dominique knows all about this. One fell on her when she was sunbathing in Kenya and broke a bone in her back. She is lucky to be alive!

All the other passengers on the little boat which took us out to Glovers Reef stayed in comfortable 'over the water' cabins on stilts and ate their meals in the one little restaurant on the island. We couldn't afford to eat out so all our supplies had to come across with us from the mainland in two cardboard boxes. Mum was rushed and didn't get enough time to shop properly in the tiny village shop meaning that she didn't buy enough food for the week. Their staple diet consisted of baked beans and eggs for seven days by which time the novelty of being reunited with baked beans in Belize was well and truly over. Fortunately I didn't have to spend too much time in the tent with them!

Because of my new friends I was invited for sleepovers nearly every night and ate fresh sea food and cakes at the restaurant.

After a few days of eating nothing but baked beans and coconut rice Mum (or 'Hungrid') was getting grumpy. In addition to being permanently hungry there was a swamp in the middle of the island which attracted thousands of biting mosquitoes especially in the evenings. While this didn't affect the 'over the water' cabin dwellers, who nearly always had the benefit of a sea breeze, for Mum and Dad camping on the sand amongst the trees there was no escape. Although Mum slathered on the most powerful insect repellent she could buy, by the end of the week her arms and legs looked like she was suffering from some kind of pox. She said that she was glad that she had made the decision to buy malaria tablets for us all since leaving Mexico as it was impossible to avoid getting bitten and none of us had suffered any noticeable side effects from the medication.

The lady who runs the resort was so happy for her daughter to have a friend like me for company that she asked us to stay on the island for another week free of charge. However we were keen to be back on our bikes and well on the way through Central America before the rainy season really kicked in. Also Mum wanted to be able to look back on the week as a holiday in a tropical paradise as opposed to a stint in the jungle on 'I'm a celebrity, get me out of here!' On the last couple of days she had found herself eyeing up the woodlice on the walls of the cooking shed and thinking that they would probably taste OK if she boiled them up and added plenty of ketchup!

Terrified in Tegucigalpa

To cross to Honduras from Belize we had to take a boat called the D Express. The two hour journey was very bumpy and the passengers were thrown around. Mum and I were both sick. After trailing around the streets of Puerto Cortez for miles, in search of the immigration office, we spent a night in a room which we shared with several giant cockroaches. They were the biggest I had ever seen.

The road from the port took us uphill into the misty cloud forests where for a while the air felt cooler. We cycled up to a huge lake called Lago Johoa where we stopped at a waterside restaurant for fresh bass and chips which were made from plantains instead of potatoes.

Honduras is one of the world's biggest importers of bananas. Hundreds of banana stalls were dotted along the sides of the roads. My favourite thing about Honduras was the abundance of beautiful flowers. Many of the walls and hedges are covered with bougainvillea bushes full of dazzling pink, purple, crimson and white blossoms which make even the shabbiest looking old shacks look exotic.

We found the people of Honduras extremely friendly and helpful but they kept warning us about how dangerous it was here which was quite unsettling. Nearly every person we chatted to eventually asked the question 'Have you been mugged yet?' as though it was only a matter of time before we were attacked and abandoned on the side of the road, stripped of all our worldly possessions.

They advised us to be especially careful while travelling through the capital city of Tegucigalpa and not under any circumstances to be caught out on the streets at night. With this in mind we planned to get there early but we hadn't accounted for two long steep hills on the outskirts of town and, as we made our way towards the centre we hit the heavy traffic congestion of rush hour. Then it went dark!

There were no street lights or shoulder to cycle on. Fast traffic thundered past us nearly hitting us. We tried to find our way to the downtown part of the city where the hostels were but there were no signs and our map made so little sense that it might have been of a completely different city. We approached taxi drivers for directions but they couldn't help us either.

We were exhausted and very scared. We had done the one thing that everybody had advised us against which was to get lost in Tegucigalpa at night! I was very cross with my parents because we had come across a hostel in a small village fifteen miles away from the city and I had wanted to stop there but they decided to press on and now we were in a pickle.

We pulled into a McDonalds to escape from the crazy night streets and to gather our thoughts. The staff and customers could see that we were stressed and did everything that they could to help us. They told us that we were in a bad part of town and that it wasn't safe for us to go back out

again. They advised us to get a taxi to a hotel but the tiny city cabs had no room for bikes and trailers and we couldn't just leave them.

One of the customers who had overheard our conversation, offered to call his cousin who worked in a hotel in the town centre. He was pretty sure that they had a minibus which would take our gear. He said that it was reasonably clean and comfortable and would probably be suitable for us.

We gratefully accepted. While we were waiting for the taxi, he explained how he had recently been held at gunpoint by a gang and forced to withdraw all his money from a teller and hand it over to them. This happened just around the corner from the McDonalds and he was a local, not a tourist like us!

We got a bit of a shock when we arrived at the hotel though. It turned out to be an Intercontinental, one of a chain of upmarket, flashy hotels used for business conferences and meetings. It was by far the poshest hotel that we had ever stayed in, costing us fifteen times more than what we usually spent on a night's accommodation but by then we were so relieved to be inside that we didn't care.

We stood there in the gleaming foyer feeling very out of place in our torn filthy clothes, comparing our shabby pile of dry bags with the personalised matching suitcases wheeled along by the other customers. A receptionist in a smart suit filled out our details before a porter in a white uniform accompanied us up the mirrored lifts to our room.

The room was huge and air conditioned with thick mattresses, luxuriously clean starched white sheets and a bath. There were no ant trails or cockroaches, not even one!

In the morning we sat down for an 'All you can eat' buffet breakfast where we found every breakfast thing we had ever heard of. Dad ate without stopping for two hours.

On our way out of the city, which once again involved pedalling up a long, steep hill, a group of young lads surrounded us and started pushing us around and demanding money. Mum smacked one of them and made a loud growling noise. Dad began to give them a stern lecture (in English) about how they ought to be ashamed of themselves for harassing a family with a small child. After that they backed off.

When we arrived at the next town we realised that we had left our Lonely Planet guidebook in the hotel drawer. Two lovely people called Laura and Dan rode all the way back on their motorbikes to fetch it for us. In the evenings they took us out on the back of the bikes to a restaurant for enchiladas.

In Nicaragua we joined a road named Ruta Colonial y de los Volcanos. There are a lot of volcanoes in Nicaragua, many of which are active with smoke puffing from the craters.

In Masaya we met up with Sue and Martin, two English cyclists who were also touring the Americas on their bikes. We teamed up with them to climb to the summit of Volcan Masaya which is the most active volcano in Nicaragua. From the top we could look right down into the crater where thick clouds of acrid smoke were being belched out. It reminded us of Mount Doom in Mordor especially as there was a thunder and lightning storm going on at the same time. Apparently in the old days people were thrown into the crater as a sacrifice to appease the 'hag' of the volcano.

Mum followed a little path around to the other side in the hope of getting a view of some red lava but she was escorted back by two park rangers wearing gas masks who told her that it was unsafe to breathe the air there. The lava in the volcano can only be seen when it is dark.

Sue, who is a real maths teacher, gave me some lessons while we were staying in Granada together and taught me all about equivalent fractions and decimals.

We all cycled together to Granada, another beautiful colonial city where the houses are painted in different colours and horses pull traps through the narrow streets. There was some kind of parade taking place in the centre. Crowds of people were singing and following a big statue of Jesus which was being carried along the road.

Nicaragua is beautiful but there is a lot of poverty. There was an earthquake and a terrible war there a few years ago. More than 40% of the young people are unemployed. Many people have less than $2 a day to survive on and it made us sad to see children, elderly people and people in wheelchairs having to beg to make a living. It made us feel very lucky to live where we do in our comfortable home in a safe country.

By the time we crossed the border into Costa Rica, the climate was becoming extremely hot and humid. We found that we could cope with it on our bikes during the day but at night the heat was stifling. Sometimes we felt as if we could barely breathe. In the tent we had to take turns to fan one another with maps and mop each other's faces with a wet cloth. If we had a room we took frequent cold showers throughout the night and lay down close to the fan. Sometimes we showered with our clothes on just so that we would stay cool for a little bit longer.

It was May and the rainy season was underway. Every day began bright and clear. As the morning went on it became unbearably hot and sultry. By midday the clouds built up, thunder began to rumble and it was a relief when a few big drops of rain began to splash onto our faces. For a few hours every afternoon thunder crashed and streaks of lightning ripped across the sky while a deluge of torrential rain turned the roads into rivers. By evening the sun had broken through once more, the sky cleared and soon everything was dry again.

Soon after entering Costa Rica we left the main road and turned east into the hills, climbing up a steep winding road to Arenal National Park to see Volcan Arenal, the country's most active volcano. People are not permitted to hike up to the summit of this mountain because the crater constantly spits out big chunks of lava.

The best time to view the volcano is after dark so once we had set up camp we cycled for ten miles along a dirt track to a viewpoint. At first all that we could see were clouds of smoke and ash rolling down the slopes of the volcano. As night fell the lava began to glow and form flaming streaks of red light on the mountainside.

At night from our campsite we could hear the constant rumbling and clattering of rocks tumbling down from above. It sounded very close and I don't think I would have been comfortable spending too many nights there.

After watching the volcano from the viewpoint on the first night I suddenly felt very tired and we were all dreading cycling back ten miles along the dirt track in the dark to get to our campsite. Luckily Ed, one of the photographers there, very kindly gave us a lift in his tiny little car even though his own lodgings were in the opposite direction. As there was no room for the bikes, he came and fetched us the next day so we could pick them up. He took us bird watching in the mountain jungle near Arenal. Through his big telephoto lens we got some great views of a pair of brightly coloured keel billed toucans perched at the top of a tall tree.

After Arenal we continued to head inland and uphill to the winter home of two Canadians called Janet and Bob. Although they had never met us, they had invited us to stay for a few days because Brad, the motorcyclist from the Dempster Highway was a good friend of theirs and he had told them about our journey.

Pursued by the Paparazzi!

Getting to the town of Grecia was more of a challenge than we had bargained for. Some of the hills were so steep that it took all three of us to push one bike and trailer up the road. It was worth it when we arrived. Janet and Bob were lovely and spoiled us rotten, helping us to recharge our batteries for the next stage of the journey.

On the way back to the coast, three people pulled up next to us, saying that they had been looking out for us. They had seen the article which Janet had written about us in the Tico Times and wanted to meet us. Michael was once a photographer for the tabloid newspapers in Britain and was interested in interviewing us. They took us out for a fabulous lunch, asked me lots of questions and took pictures of us on the bike. Later that month there was a big article about us in the Scottish Daily Record!

We enjoyed reading the online copy although Mum was a bit alarmed when she read that, according to the reporter, we were on a 30,000 mile journey. She had based her calculations on the assumption that the whole distance was 16,500 miles. If the newspaper had got it right we still had another 23,000 miles to go! I would be a teenager by the time we arrived at our final destination!

We were looking for a place to pitch the tent one night. In the distance we could see a bridge across a wide river. As we approached we could make out a flat green grassy area on the banks of each side of the slowly flowing water and we wondered if it might be a suitable spot to camp. We stopped on the bridge and leaned over the railings to get a better view. There, beneath the road, sunbathing next to the murky water were about twenty big crocodiles. No it was definitely not a sensible place to camp!

On the other side of the river at the village of Tarcoles we spotted a hotel. At $35 it would send us way over budget but there was only an hour before darkness fell. The choice between spending $35 dollars on a nice room and pitching our tent on a croc infested river bank was not a difficult one.

Soon even Dad, who has a tendency to sulk when we are

Sean and Ingrid take Kate, 9, on bike odyssey from Alaska to Argentina..

30,000-MILE SCHOOL RUN

By Denise Watson

forced to overspend, was glad that we had opted to stay there. In the evening two big blue, yellow and red birds flew overhead. When we asked the receptionists what type they were, she said 'Lapa Roja' which is the name for a scarlet macaw. At dusk about fifty of them flew over in pairs squawking loudly.

The next morning there was a loud racket coming from the park next to the hotel. We grabbed our cameras and hurried over to the big old almond trees where a large number of the parrots were settled, breaking up the nuts and dropping the shells on our heads. One macaw even dropped one of its feathers onto me which I kept to put in my project file.

We felt very privileged to have had an experience like this. We hadn't expected to get a sighting of a scarlet macaw in the wild. Their population has decreased drastically in the last century as a result of deforestation and the pet trade. Although they are now a protected species, much of their habitat has been destroyed and large areas of tropical rain forest continue to be cleared in Central America to make way for agriculture and industry.

We hiked through a protected area of rainforest in Manuel Antonio National Park. Huge morph butterflies with shimmering wings floated by. Lethargic three toed sloths hung from branches, their movements very slow, unlike the squirrel monkeys which we saw taking big leaps from branch to branch almost as if they were flying. Groups of white faced monkeys came down really close when we were eating our picnic. One was running around with a tiny baby wrapped around its neck. Its little face looked human as it peeped back at is over its mother's shoulder.

For the rest of our journey through Costa Rica we hugged the surf battered coastline, stopping to pick up juicy ripe mangoes which fell from the trees and rolled into piles on the road. Iguanas, giant armoured lizards which looked like prehistoric beasts wandered slowly across the road.

Arrested by the Police in Panama – Twice!

Being in Panama in May felt like being in the steam room at the swimming pool all the time! We were either soaked with rain or drenched in sweat day and night. Dry just didn't come into it. Even my teddy bears got BO.

Every day there were huge tropical storms with multiple streaks of forked lightning and thunderclaps so loud that we could feel the noise vibrating through our bodies. The rain was sometimes so thick that we could barely see in front of us and we had to wade through ankle deep water as we pushed our bikes along the road. A lot of our time in Panama was spent huddled together in leaky bus shelters waiting for the rain to ease.

It was very uncomfortable inside the tent at night. We camped on a beach one night and Mum decided to try and sleep in a hammock that was strung between two trees. She said that she could feel the breeze on her face which was very refreshing compared to the suffocating heat inside the tent but she kept being woken up by things crawling over her face.

The rainforests of Central and South America are home to a large number of venomous snakes and spiders. One of the world's most deadly spiders, the phoneutria or wandering banana spider, is fairly common in lowland Panama, especially at night. It is sometimes found in fruit or piles of leaves or even in shoes or clothes which have been left outside.

In our guidebook, at the end of each chapter, there is always a section telling you about all the dangerous creatures you may encounter or the diseases that you are at risk of picking up in that particular area. We decided that we much preferred reading the 'Dangers and Annoyances' part after we had left that country safely behind us. In other words, ignorance is bliss!

The cost of rooms was still outside our budget but as camping was so uncomfortable we occasionally splashed out.

One night we found a room for fifteen dollars. It was dirty and full of junk that was heaped up around one small bed with barely enough space for the three of us to squeeze into. As we were settling in, Mum felt something sharp scratching her leg. When we looked more closely we saw that there were jagged, rusty bed springs protruding from the material right in the centre of the mattress.

Every ten years in Panama there is a census. Nobody is allowed to travel anywhere until they have been given a ticket to prove that they have been counted and that all their information has been recorded. That includes everyone in the country on that day, even the tourists like us.

The 2010 census happened to take place when we were there. We tried to get to a hotel the night before but we couldn't find one so we ended up camping on the side of the road in a grassy field which was probably heaving with wandering banana spiders and God knows what else.

Next morning the roads were completely clear of traffic. This is because all the sane people were in their homes waiting to fill their census forms in. It was illegal for us to be out on the road but we couldn't face another day and night camping in the same field so we set out towards the next village enjoying the unusual peace of the empty highway.

Eventually we were stopped by the police. We had to sit in a bus shelter with them in the power shower like rain for hours while we waited for the man with the official papers to arrive. By the time he time he had got out of his car and scurried across the road to the bus shelter, the sheets of paper had turned to pulp and Mum and Dad had difficulty writing anything legible.

The police were very friendly and apologetic for making us stay with them for so long. They shared their fruit drinks with me and we made tuna sandwiches for them. They showed us photos of their kids on their phones. One of them, Kempton was the champion wrestler for the whole of Central

America. He made me laugh by showing me how he could wiggle both his ears.

Oh and by the way, I know the population of Panama in 2010. It was 3.672 million including the three of us!

We crossed the Panama Canal, a manmade stretch of water which was constructed about a hundred years ago so that trading ships carrying cargo could cross from the Pacific Ocean to the Atlantic and vice versa without having to sail all the way around South America. The canal is only 50 miles long. This part of the American continent is so narrow that even we were able to cycle from the Pacific to the Atlantic in one day.

We were in trouble once again when the police saw us cycling across the bridge. Apparently there is a sign saying 'No Cyclists.' We wondered what other cyclists normally do when they want to get to the other side. Were we supposed to swim across?

We were allowed to camp next to the office headquarters in Soberania National Park where we had the use of a toilet and a hosepipe to cool ourselves down. While we were there we walked some of the rainforest trails and got glimpses of many beautiful birds such as toucans, trogons, blue headed parrots, Montezuma oropendola and red headed manekens. Our best views of the keel billed toucans with their vibrant plumage and beaks were from a viewing post on one of these paths.

It is not possible to cycle from Panama to Colombia because there is no road for sixty miles. Between the road heads in each country there is an area of dense rainforest and swamp known as the Darien Gap. It has a reputation of being extremely dangerous. Cyclists have the choice of flying from Panama City or hitching a ride with a boat.

At the time there was no ferry but while we were staying at a hostel named 'The Purple House' which was painted purple inside and outside, we found out about a hostel

named 'Wunderbar' near the city of Colon. The owners help to arrange transport for people who wish to travel by sea to Cartagena in Colombia.

Our boat was a yacht called the Minorca and our Captains were Steven from France and Sara from Colombia. Besides us there was a French couple names Clarisse and Enrique who also had a tandem.

We were very lucky with the deal that we got. We were given a lovely comfortable cabin of our own with three beds at the front of the boat. Sara made delicious meals with lots of fresh fruit and salad and fish caught from the yacht while we were on board.

For two days we anchored amongst the San Blas Islands. There are over two hundred small islands about ten miles off the coast of Panama fringed with palm trees and white sand Many are uninhabited. Some are home to the Kuna people who have lived here for hundreds of years.

We were taken on a tour of a Kuna village where the women wear the most amazing clothes I have ever seen. They have bright headscarves and colourful patterned skirts down to their knees. Their blouses are decorated around the middle with the Molas which is the traditional craftwork for which the Kuna people are best known. They are made by embroidering geometrical patterns and animal designs onto squares of cloth. They are very pretty and we were pleased that there were some for sale.

The ladies also have strings of tiny beads wrapped tightly around their arms and legs to make patterns. There is a line painted down the middle of their faces and big gold rings in their noses between the nostrils rather than at one side. The men wear jeans and T Shirts.

Our guide showed us around a Kuna house. The walls are made from thin bamboo sticks laced together vertically and the roofs thatched with palm leaves. In this particular house fourteen people lived together in one big room, sleeping in

hammocks. The people travel from one island to another in dug out canoes using a wooden paddle or a pole to propel their boats in the shallow water. While we were anchored out families came out in their boats to sell their Molas. Mum and I had beads wrapped around our arms.

We went snorkelling again above the coral reefs. A group of dolphins jumped and danced around the bow of our boat and one night a pod of orcas surfaced in the moonlight. The whole experience was so romantic that Enrique proposed to Clarisse and they got engaged. Sara brought out wine and home made chocolate cake to celebrate the happy occasion.

Our journey at sea lasted six days. On the morning of the last day the dazzling clear waters of the Caribbean gradually became more murky, boat traffic increased and we could slowly begin to make out the skyscrapers of the city of Cartagena appearing on the skyline.

CHAPTER 7

COLOMBIA AND ECUADOR

The Tomlinsons turn into Telly Slobs

We stayed in Cartagena for three days preparing for the next stage and exploring the city. The old part of the town is still surrounded by a big stone wall and forts which were built in the 16th century to protect it from pirates and attacks from outsiders. There were tall old buildings and churches whichever way we looked. Balconies dripping with flowers hung over the narrow cobbled streets.

At night the centre was dimly lit with old fashioned lamps Men sat around the plazas in pairs playing chess. The air was full of the smells of food from outdoor stands. We bought the empanadas which are like a pasty filled with egg, potatoes or mince. Often they are yellow because the flour is made from corn. We tried *arepas*, a flat round maize pancake which we had with butter and the local cheese.

The mission to find nice cheese had become a top priority amongst the Tomlinson's. We are a cheese loving family but once we left the USA we rarely saw cheddar as we knew it. We could often buy the sliced, plastic wrapped, processed cheese singles in shops and Gouda or Edam was usually to be found in supermarkets in the cities but we never really got used

to the locally produced cheese which we found in the rural areas. It was spongy in texture and very salty but without much of a cheesy flavour. It smelt a bit like Dad's socks, hence the reason we called it 'sock cheese'

Not long after leaving Cartagena we began to climb up and up to join the Andes, a famous range of mountains which is around six thousand miles long and stretches all the way down the western side of South America from Columbia in the north to Chile in the south. Its snow capped peaks rise to over 6000 metres above sea level. To the west of the Andes, along the Pacific coastline, dry, sandy desert stretches for thousands of miles. To the east is the Amazon Basin, a vast tropical rain forest through which the mighty Amazon River runs.

It was a relief to finally escape from the oppressive heat at sea level. For the first time in months we had to dig out our fleece jackets which had been buried at the bottom of our clothes bags.

In the past Colombia has had a reputation for being a dangerous place to travel. Mum and Dad were on edge to begin with, half expecting a gun toting guerrilla or knife wielding terrorist to leap out from behind a bush. However, in our experience it turned out to be one of the safest and most cycle friendly countries that we visited. Other cyclist tourists that we met felt the same way.

Cycling is Colombia's most popular sport besides football and at the weekends the roads were filled with cyclists dressed in bright technicolour racing gear, all going much faster than us. It was a good place to have bike trouble as there was always somebody close at hand who was equipped and willing to help us fix it.

Wherever we went people clapped and cheered or gave us the thumbs up sign. They shouted 'Bien Viaje' (Good Journey), 'Suerte' (Good Luck), 'Bienvenidos' (Welcome) and 'Que Linda!' (How Sweet!). For some reason they often called us 'Mono' which means monkey. We're not quite sure why.

In Colombia many of the restaurants had a sign outside advertising *Almuerzo*. This means that there is a set lunch which, costing around two dollars, was much cheaper than ordering different dishes from off the menu. It usually starts with a big bowl of soup and is followed by a simple meal of rice, beans, plantains and some kind of meat, most commonly chicken. Sometimes a drink or dessert is included in the price.

Now that we had discovered the *Almuerzo* option, it meant that we could finally afford to eat in restaurants and we got into a routine of cycling about twenty miles, breaking up the day with a cooked lunch then continuing to our destination where we would buy bread and something to go with it to eat in the evening once we were settled in to our tent or room. This system worked well for us throughout Colombia, Ecuador and Peru.

Choosing the set lunch meant that Dad, who was vegetarian, had to start eating chicken because the meal always included some kind of meat. Even vegetable soup invariably had hen's feet or head or some body part floating around in it somewhere.

In Colombia a popular soup was a meaty broth containing vegetables and plantains known as *Sancocho*. Sometimes we were served *Caldo de Gallina* (chicken soup) and one day we had *Sopa de Mondongo* which contains tripe. Mum liked it but I wasn't very keen.

In Colombia, Ecuador and Peru accommodation was cheaper than it had been in Central America. Rooms in *Residentiales* and *Hospedajes* cost between ten and fifteen dollars a night which meant that we could afford to take a break from camping every night.

Even the most basic of rooms came with a television, often cable, which meant that we got to watch programmes in

English such as Friends, The Big Bang Theory and Desperate Housewives.

Now when you have been out on a bike all day in the heat and the dust and the traffic, getting lost, shopping, ordering meals and asking for directions in a foreign language, by the time you have arrived at your destination you can sometimes feel that you have been immersed in local culture quite enough. Often all Dad and I wanted to do was to shut ourselves in our room with a big bag of grub, away from the stress and noise of the outside world and watch mentally unchallenging sitcoms in English.

Mum, however, had other ideas. She seemed to be on a mission to tick off every single tourist attraction in her Lonely Planet guide.

'There'll be plenty of time to watch telly when we get home' she nagged at us. One night Dad and I were concentrating on America's Next Top Model, our eyes fixed to the screen, trying to ignore Mum who was rambling on about some hike to an obscure overgrown ruin that she was planning to drag us out on, when a trailer came on for the next episode of The Mentalist, an American police drama. Mum stopped reciting from the Lonely Planet.

'Who's that man?' she asked, referring to the main character, (admittedly quite good looking for an old person), followed shortly by 'Now that looks interesting. Why don't we watch that?'

Our problem was solved! After one episode of The Mentalist the Lonely Planet guidebook was cast aside and forgotten. Mum was now every bit as keen as we were to gain access to the Warner Brother's channel. In fact sometimes we ended up cycling ten miles further than usual to stay at a *Hospedaje*, just so Mum could get her Patrick fix!

As we cycled along we kept an eye out for the *Jugos Naturales* signs outside shops and restaurants. There were a variety of exotic tropical fruit to choose from such as mango, *guayaba*, *lulo*, *guanabana*, *maracuya* (passion fruit) and *mora* (Andean blackberry). Whichever fruits we picked were squeezed into a big glass while we watched. Our favourite of them all was mango.

In each country that we visited, Mum tried to make sure that we had some experience of at least one thing for which that particular nation was famous. For example in Canada we viewed glaciers, visited 1st Nation village sites and learned about the gold rush. In the US it was the geological and geographical wonders of regions such as Yellowstone and Arches National Parks. In Mexico the turtles on the beaches and the Mayan ruins were part of my project. In Central America volcanoes, coral atolls and the wildlife of the tropical rainforests were amongst the main attractions.

Having studied the guidebook carefully to find out what features Colombia is especially well known for, she announced that we could try one of the following three things:

The world's best quality cocaine (Dad's choice)

Surgical breast enhancements (Mum's choice)

Visiting a coffee plantation

We opted for option number 3 as it was the only one compatible with our £20 a day budget. Option 1 is illegal and might have resulted in a prison sentence. Option 2 would have used the whole of the rest of our travel funds and would have only paid for one boob.

Colombia is the world's second biggest producer of coffee after Brazil. Our route through Colombia followed the Autopista del Café, (the Coffee Highway) through the Zona Cafetera. We passed many coffee plantations on the slopes above the road, where the red berries, known as coffee cherries, were just beginning to ripen. The beans are harvested from these berries during the dry season.

In the lowland areas we passed miles and miles of sugar cane fields. Lorries pulling four or five wagons overflowing with cane thundered past.

In Popayan, where the old colonial buildings are nearly all painted white, we stopped to look at the square and we were instantly surrounded by a large crowd of people. A man was pointing a TV camera at us and someone else held a microphone up to Mum's face and began firing questions at her in rapid Spanish. They told us that the interview would be shown on Colombian News that evening but we never got to see it (probably because we spent too much of the evening tuned into the Warner Brothers channel.)

As we got closer to the border of Ecuador some of the hills we had to climb were so long that we were crawling uphill all day long. In Ecuador we went from near sea level to over 3000 metres and back again many times without any flat ground in between. Rather than following the valleys, which would have been more gradual, the road south through Ecuador seemed to go straight across the mountain ranges from one valley to the next.

On the day before we left Colombia the road zigzagged into the heavy drizzle and mist above precipitous drops and through several long dark tunnels. Goats and sheep, grazing unseen on the cliffs above, dislodged loose rocks which tumbled down from the fog, sometimes narrowly missing us. This was quite worrying considering the size of the small boulders we saw scattered over the tarmac. Although we were cold, wet and tired we thought it would be wise to press on until we were out of the danger zone.

Villages, Volcanoes and Violent Vomiting

On June 30th, after a week in Ecuador, we arrived at the equator. Near the village of Cayembe there is a line carved in the ground showing the exact position of the imaginary zero degrees line around the centre of the earth. We could walk from the Tropic of Cancer in the northern hemisphere, across the line, to the tropic of Capricorn in a single step!

The monument there is really a giant sun dial. It was hollow in the centre and inside, at the base, was a mirror. The guide explained how, twice a year, for one hour the sun reflects directly into the mirror. This happens during the spring and autumn equinoxes when the earth is vertical in relation to the sun.

Mum was hoping that the water in the washbasin would go down the plug hole in the opposite direction now we were in a different hemisphere because of the Coriolis Effect but after trying out a few different sinks, she still couldn't really tell whether the water was flowing anticlockwise or not.

Although equatorial regions are generally the hottest places on earth because of their close proximity to the sun, it was quite chilly here because we were already at an altitude of 3000 metres.

As we were leaving the town of Pifo we were joined by a small boy who started talking to us. He said that he was ten; the same age as me, although he looked much younger. He asked if he could have a ride on the bike so I jumped off and Sean rode around with him on the back for a little while. But when Sean said that it was time for us to leave, he clung to the bike, refusing to get off. He said that he wanted to come with us and be part of our family. We said that we were sorry but we couldn't take him and gave him some of our sandwiches and biscuits in case he was hungry. He wouldn't eat anything and continued to hold onto the bike.

We asked him where he lived and where his parents were. He pointed back down the hill. We gave him some money so that he could get a bus back to his home but he didn't accept that either. He just continued to follow us.

We were worried about him but had no idea how to handle the situation. In the end we turned back towards the outskirts of the town until we found a group of workmen mending the road. We explained our predicament as well as we could with our limited Spanish and fortunately one of the

workers knew the boy's family and said that we could leave him with them and they would make sure he got home.

We found the encounter quite distressing, feeling similar to the way we had when stray dogs had tried to befriend us and we had had to leave them behind. We were not able, with our basic knowledge of Spanish, to judge what was really happening. It is likely that Spanish might not have even been his first language. He might have just been naughty and looking for a bit of an adventure or he might have been in some kind of trouble.

We had heard that many of the indigenous people of the Andes are suspicious of white people because they believe that they sometimes abduct children so they can sell them for body parts or for other evil purposes. We certainly did not wish to be mistaken for kidnappers and knew it would be unwise for us to get involved but we felt sad and guilty that we had abandoned him. Since then we often wondered if there was more we could have done.

Ecuador's two highest peaks, Chimborazo, 6310 metres, and Cotopaxi, 5897 metres are both volcanoes. To camp in Cotopaxi National Park we had to climb for twenty five kilometres up a steep, bumpy track and push the bikes across a river. By midday it was pouring with rain and the bikes felt very heavy on the soft ground.

By the time we got to 3800 metres we were soaking and shivering. I was slightly queasy possibly because of the altitude. The visitor centre and café there, where we had hoped to shelter and buy snacks, were closed so we pitched our tent on the grass nearby. There was no sign of the mountain. We were all feeling a bit fed up. Mum and Dad were arguing about whose idea it had been to waste time and money by making such a difficult detour in rubbish weather.

The locals here chew coca leaves. Mum brewed up some coca leaf tea which is known to be a remedy for altitude sickness.

Next morning the sky was completely clear and Cotopaxi was in full view. As the sun rose, the snow and icicles near the summit glistened with first pink and then golden light. We left the trailers next to the tent and rode our unladen bikes past flower filled meadows to Laguna de Limpiopungo where the mountain was mirrored perfectly in the glassy water.

Cotopaxi is still slightly active and we could see little puffs of smoke drifting out from one of the craters. There was a hut near the lagoon where we camped the following night. There was a fireplace inside the hut where we eventually managed to get a very smoky fire going with the damp wood that we found. We saw no other people all the time we were there but we did get a good view of an Andean fox which came very close to the building. We thought that it was a wolf because it looked like a cross between a fox and a big Alsatian dog.

Guinea Pig is a very popular dish in Ecuador. We often passed roasting machines with about six of them turning around on spits. One day when we couldn't find a restaurant serving *almuerzo*, we decided to give it a try. It arrived on a big plate complete with head, claws and whiskers. We expected it to taste like chicken but it didn't. It was a bit fishy and slimy and we could hardly find any meat on it. I thought it tasted like chewing on an old slipper. The waiter told us that the local people eat the whole thing but I really couldn't imagine how that was possible.

Whole pigs roasting on big barbecues on the side of the road was another common sight in Ecuador. This is where we bought fritadas, another national dish with pieces of fried pork, fried potatoes and roasted corn.

Considering all the diseases that can potentially be picked up in the tropics, our family got off quite lightly. On the whole the three of us managed to stay healthy throughout the time that we were away. The one exception to this was when Mum got food poisoning in Ecuador. We never worked out exactly

what it was that Mum ate but one minute she was fine and the next she was so incapacitated by sickness that she couldn't even make it down to the next village a few miles down the road. We just had to squeeze the tent onto a patch of weedy gravel in a tiny lay-by while Mum crouched on her hands and knees, vomiting uncontrollably for two days. Even when there was no food or liquid left inside she could not stop retching. She thought her stomach was turning inside out. She couldn't even manage the tiniest bit of water without throwing it back up again.

It wasn't pretty I can tell you. Anyone who has had the experience of being with my Mum when she is carsick will appreciate what I am saying. She makes the loudest most revolting retching sounds of anybody I have ever met.

After the second night Mum thought she might be fit to get to the next village but after a very short distance she just wobbled off her bike and collapsed onto the ground, groaning and puking. Once again we were forced to pitch our tent in the middle of nowhere underneath a bridge.

We all agreed that the low point of the whole journey was when Mum, between sick noises, suggested to Dad that he should do some homework with me. I was on a chapter in my Wizard Whimstaff book, either Smelly Spelling or Gruesome Grammar, which was looking at English words derived from different countries.

It really wasn't making a great deal of sense to me and my concentration, not surprisingly, was not at its best. Dad was getting increasingly cross as the more he attempted to explain the point of the exercise, the less I understood it.

After a few wild guesses at the answer to question 7 (pasta eaten with a tomato sauce) to which I replied 'Beans?, Onions?, Pizza?' Dad lost patience altogether.

'It's spaghetti you stupid idiot!' he yelled.
After that we decided that it was best if my homework was left to Mum, and Dad stuck to fixing the bikes.

The next night Mum wasn't feeling so good again. We found a room for $15 but it turned out to be another one of those love motels. Dad managed to persuade the owner to let us stay on the understanding that we didn't switch the telly on. We were locked in and guarded by two fierce dogs which patrolled the yard outside, barking and growling.

The room was amazing. It had one giant soft bed, mirrors on the ceiling and a Jacuzzi bathroom with coloured lights that faded in and out.

'Look Mum! The bed's got an electric blanket!' I squealed. But it turned out to be a gadget to make the bed vibrate.
Not bad for $15! Our very own theme park!

The Andean people are well known for their craftwork, especially their colourful weavings made from sheep and llama wool. In the mountains most villages have a weekly market where they gather to sell and trade their produce and crafts. We loved the markets in Ecuador. When we were in Otavalo we visited the Plaza del Ponchos where there is a huge craft market.

Markets are a great place to see the indigenous people of Ecuador wearing traditional dress which differs from one village to the next. The women of Otavalo wear white blouses with flowers embroidered around them and big lacy frills on the neck and sleeves. They have long black skirts and shawls and pieces of cloth folded over their heads. The men wear long blue ponchos and top hats. Their sandals are made from rope. Their hair is tied back in a long plait.

When we got to Latacunga we took the bus up to the big Thursday morning market in Saquisili. Most of the women there were wearing brightly coloured tasselled shawls of turquoise, pink, red or orange. They have knee length skirts which are often velvet with embroidery along the bottom. Nearly all the women wear felt pork pie hats, sometimes with a peacock feather. One old lady was wearing a very traditional outfit of pink with a bowler hat and was holding a bobbin. Underneath her hand woven shawl she was wearing a T shirt with Hannah Montana written across the front!

There were so many beautiful things for sale that Mum found it hard to resist the urge to buy things for our house but the bikes were already too heavily laden. In Saquisili she could no longer resist the temptation and she bought two paintings and a weaving from a lady from Otavalo. The weaving was made from alpaca and took her a week to make. It only cost $18! The postage home, on the other hand, was $60 but it arrived safely and now hangs above our fireplace, brightening up the living room.

Most of the time the high mountains of Ecuador were obscured by thick cloud but on the morning we left Riobamba, Chimborazo, Ecuador's highest peak, was clear for a while and we got a great view of its snowy summit behind Calpi Cathedral.

The countryside between the villages was a patchwork of little fields of crops, grass and flowers. The landscape was dotted with people, mainly women in colourful shawls and ponchos, labouring on the land, some with hoes, others carrying big bundles on their backs or herding animals.

The indigenous people of the Andes of Peru, Ecuador and Bolivia are called Quechua and this is also the name of their first language although the majority can also speak Spanish. The Quechuan people have descended directly from the Incas. They make their living mainly from subsistence farming, using the terracing method to grow crops on the very steep slopes. Very little machinery is used which is why the farming is so labour intensive. Sometimes we saw pairs of oxen pulling a yoke, steered by one man to plough the earth. One of the staple crops here is quinoa, a cereal with high nutritional value which grows well in the harsh mountain conditions found in the Andes.

Reaching the 10,000 miles mark was a momentous occasion for us. As we cycled along Sean called out the numbers

from 9999.7, 9999.8, 9999.9 ....Drum roll ....
Our milometer went back to zero! It didn't go up to five figure numbers. What an anticlimax! By the end of our journey it read 6600 which really meant 16600 but as it often stopped working whenever it rained it's likely that our actual mileage was quite a bit higher.

CHAPTER 8

PERU

Friends for the Teddy Bears

Just after we crossed the border between Ecuador and Peru we met Harry from Holland and Ivana from Argentina. They were cycling from Prudhoe Bay to Ushuaia, visiting every single country in the Americas on their route. Harry, who has already climbed to the summit of the highest mountains in all seven continents, was aiming to reach the top of the highest peak in each country that they cycled through. We decided to team up for a day or two. We ended up cycling together for three months!

We met quite a lot of cycle tourists on our journey, some of whom were making similar journeys to ourselves. Usually after camping for a night together or sharing a meal and swapping stories they zoomed on ahead. We clicked straight away with Harry and Ivana and they didn't mind cycling at our slow pace.

For the first time we had some friends to travel with. Harry had a laptop with a whole library of films on it which they put on for me in the evenings. Their favourite films were Madagascar 1 and 2.

Harry and Ivana had teddy bears of their own called

Pablo and Pedrito so Otter, Floppy and Patchit had some like minded pals to hang out with. Pablo had been to the top of Mount Everest with Harry and I think Otter secretly quite liked him. On Pedrito's birthday night we arranged a disco for all the teddies with cakes and hats and party games like pass the parcel and musical statues and everybody danced. Ivana helped me to make smart clothes for our teddies out of an old top.

They were fluent in English and Spanish so we had someone to translate for us, or at least help us out when we got stuck. It was great having company for a change. Being in a group felt safer and was more fun as they made me laugh a lot. We were able to help each other see the funny side of some of the unpleasant and annoying situations which we found ourselves in from time to time such as the night we spent in a hostel optimistically named El Silencio which did NOT live up to its name!

There was a big two day carnival taking place in northern Peru. Every hostel was full. It was beginning to go dark when we came across a shabby, dilapidated old building with a sign outside saying 'Hostal El Silencio' which we assumed meant 'The Peaceful Hostel'. They still had plenty of space.

The hostel was really just a large barn separated into stalls and the partitions between the rooms had big spaces at the top and bottom. We were kept awake for the whole night by a group of drunken, rowdy old men, their chorus of raucous cackling and guffawing interspersed with bursts of phlegmy coughing, spitting and loud belches.

Every so often, during the quiet spells, in the room on the other side, an amorous couple started yelling and groaning and jumping up and down on the bed, apparently eager to share their enjoyment of each others company with everybody within a kilometre radius.

'Ooh Mum! Can we have a pillow fight too?' I asked.

'We could if we'd been given any pillows!' Mum replied

gloomily. Eventually she threw a shoe over the wall at them. It's a miracle that I haven't been scarred for life really (not by Mum's shoe but by being subjected to pornographic sound effects at the tender age of nine.) Next morning the landlord demanded $30 per room, three times more than the average price.

On the whole, however, we found both accommodation and food in Peru to be of good quality and cheap, yet another thing which made it a very pleasant country for us to explore.

In some parts of Peru there are very few cars. Everyone uses motor taxis with three wheels and a cab to sit in.

At Tucume we saw the remains of about twenty big pyramids which were built from a mixture of mud and straw called adobe around eight hundred years ago. It is thought that it was once a place of worship for the Vicus people who lived in the deserts of north Peru between 300 BC and 200 AD. Shaman healers still invoke the power of Tucume and Raya Mountain in their ceremonies and most of the locals are afraid to visit the site at night. There is very little information about the Vicus people because most of the sites have been looted by grave robbers but they are known for their pottery and copper work, examples of which we saw on display in the museum.

Outside the museum we saw two hairless dogs. Their skin was greyish and there was no fur on their bodies at all except a few hairs on their heads. I had read about the Mayans breeding this type of dog when I was working in my project on Palenque so it was interesting for me to see what they looked like in real life.

When we got to Chiclayo we had to get a bus to Trujillo in order to avoid a town called Paijan. We had been warned not to attempt to cycle through it because there is a gang of robbers on motor taxis who lie in wait for people, especially cyclists, so they can attack them and steal all their belongings.

In contrast to the highwaymen of Paijan, we found most

people in Peru to be very honest and helpful. Mum often accidentally left her camera behind in restaurants but the people who found it always chased after her with it, despite the fact that it would have been worth a lot of money to them. One lady actually got in her car and drove five miles down the road to find us to hand us back a bag which we had left behind.

In Trujillo we stayed at a place called Casa Cyclistica where a lovely man called Lucho and his family have a house especially for cyclists to stay on their journey through South America. He even helps travellers fix their bikes. He has been running it since 1985 and over a thousand cyclists have stayed there.

Lucho came to meet us at the bus station. On our first day there he had arranged a cycle race for all the kids in the area. Dad and I took part in the lap of honour. It was fun to meet other people of different nationalities doing the same thing as us.

When we left we were very grateful to Lucho for guiding us on his bike to the edge of this big city until we joined the Pan-American Highway once again. Otherwise we would probably still be there now, trying to find our way out. On the outskirts of town we spotted some enormous rats weaving their way through the heaps of garbage beside the road and decided not to camp there especially since we had just read a newspaper report about a recent deadly outbreak of bubonic plague in the nearby town of Chicama.

After Trujillo we were surrounded by thick piles of sand as the dusty road took us through a vast expanse of coastal desert. One night Sean caught a glimpse of something moving out of the corner of his eye. There was a scorpion on his pillow, next to his ear, the second to be found in the tent so far and a warning to us to be extra thorough in checking our clothes, shoes and bags before bringing them inside.

Troublesome Tunnels

After a few miles on the coast road we turned left onto a small dirt track leading to Huaraz, a small town at 3000 metres of altitude in the Cordillera Blanca range of the Andes. To get there from sea level we had to cycle 100km of very rough, rocky track, over thick loose gravel as we followed the increasingly narrow road through the precipitous Canyon del Pato gorge.

We had to cycle through more than forty unlit tunnels thirty five of which were within the same ten kilometre stretch. Some of the tunnels were very long and dark as well as being on a steep uneven slope. There was only one lane and we were afraid of being hit by one of the many buses which rattled past. We were lucky to have Harry to go ahead and stop the traffic for us while we struggled through the darkness as quickly as we could.

After five days of camping and cycling in that dusty canyon we were the filthiest that we had ever been. It was difficult to tell what colour our clothes were. Everything including our skin, nails and hair was greyish brown.

One night we found a small quarry to camp in out of view of the road. Unfortunately we didn't notice, until it was too late, that the ground was covered in small spiky white tufts, probably some kind of a windborne cactus seed. After moving the tents, poor Dad was up all night repairing punctures on our self inflating mats and picking prickles out of the groundsheet.

After the canyon we rested at Caraz, a lovely little town high in the mountains full of *panaderias* (bakeries) and *heladerias* (ice cream shops).

We visited Yungay, a town at the foot of Huascaran, Peru's highest mountain. In 1970 the whole of the old town was buried by an avalanche of rock and ice caused by a huge earthquake. Nearly twenty thousand people died. We walked

around the Campo Santo which is now a beautiful memorial garden planted in the place where the town once stood.

There was a big election coming up soon and nearly every single house and wall in Peru had political propaganda and the names of candidates written in blue and white paint upon the white washed stone.

While Harry set off to climb Huascaran, the rest of us hiked the famous Santa Cruz trek in the Cordillera Blanca. We had to carry all our food and camping gear for five days so Mum and Dad had very heavy packs. We got our water from the streams and I helped to filter it to make it safe to drink.

On the first day we had a terrifying bus ride over a high pass with steep drops and hairpin bends. We camped next to a pretty village called Huaribampa where I bought an alpaca wool hat with earflaps from a lady called Lydia.

On the way up we saw llamas and trails of *burros* (donkeys) which were carrying supplies for climbers and also for the SENSIBLE trekkers. The porters smiled at me and asked Dad if he wanted to hire a *burro* for '*la gringanita*' to ride but I was determined to walk by myself.

We camped by a small lagoon at 4000 metres and made a small fire. By dawn the tent was covered with a layer of ice. Next morning we climbed to the top of the Punta Union Pass which, at 4750 metres was the highest point of the trek. I felt a little bit dizzy and breathless because of the altitude but it was worth it when we got to the top because of the incredible views of serrated icy peaks, hanging glaciers and turquoise lagoons.

We took a detour to spend a night at the base camp for Alpamayo which is believed by many to be the world's most beautiful mountain. From the camp Mum and I hiked to a viewpoint and built inukshuks next to the lagoon.

Our feet were covered in blisters by the time we finished the trek. Mum reckoned that this was because our feet had

softened up over the last year. We were spending so much of our day cycling that we hardly ever walked anywhere anymore!

The traditional dress worn by the women in Peru is even more vibrant than in Ecuador. They wear big white bowler hats or tall sombreros, often decorated with flowers, fans or ribbons. They have frilly blouses and bright puffy knee length skirts with several layers called Polleras. From their skirts to their ankles they wear thick woollen leg warmers. Mum said that leg warmers were very fashionable when she was a teenager but they wore them over the top of drainpipe jeans.

One thing that Mum had expected to see in the Andes was the stereotypical Peruvian or Bolivian folk bands wearing ponchos and playing traditional panpipe tunes and singing about the flight of the condor. Disappointingly we never saw a single one in South America, although surprisingly there were plenty of brass bands marching about with trumpets, trombones and tubas. Every small village seemed to have one.

We have since realised that this is because the panpipe people have all moved to Great Britain where they can be seen each Saturday in all their finery in the centre of every shopping precinct in the UK, playing 'Walking in the Air' from The Snowman and 'Love is all around' by Wet Wet Wet. Mum has considered taking a photograph of them there to use in her slide shows but feels like the WHSmiths sign in the background detracts from the authenticity.

Most of the traditional Quechuan houses are made from adobe bricks. Some of the older houses still have thatched roofs but most now have red tiles. We saw the new adobe bricks drying out in the sun. In the villages when somebody needs to build a new house, it is the custom that everyone joins together and helps out.

After leaving Huaraz we cycled up an even worse track called the Pastoruri Road to see the Puya Raimondi plants. The young plants are like a big round bush with spiky leaves then they grow a seed pod which can be ten metres high and take one hundred years to grow. After the seed pod flowers it dies and turns black. They are only to be found in a few parts of the high Andes of Peru and Bolivia at an elevation of between 3000 and 4800 metres. We camped next to a group of them.

We had hoped to continue further up to the top of the pass but in the morning, snow was falling onto our tent and the surface of the road was rapidly turning white. We cycled back to the main road and up to 4100 metres, next to the Rio Santa, the river which we had been following upstream since we left the coast nearly one month ago.

We bought some local cheese and honey from the village there before cycling 120 km back down to sea level in a few hours. At the top the tarmac road was very steep with so many wiggles and hairpin bends that, from above it resembled a pile of spaghetti.

Mum arrived at the bottom of the hill about two hours later than the rest of us and was furious when I told her that our speedometer had reached fifty miles per hour. Her top speed was twenty five. It's no wonder that she got through three times as many sets of brakes than we did!

Lima, Peru's capital city is huge. It took us a whole day to cycle from the outskirts into the centre of the city and another day to cycle out to the other side. The five of us teamed up with Alicia and Alvaro from Spain who were doing a world tour on their bikes so for the next few days there were seven people in our group.

At Paracas we met the sea for the first time since we left Cartagena in Colombia, six months earlier. We took a boat trip out to the Ballestas Islands. Because they are so rich in wildlife they are known as 'the poor man's Galapagos' which was perfect for us as we couldn't afford to go to the Galapagos Islands.

The islands had some impressive archways and were

covered with sea birds. On the boat trip we saw sea lions, dolphins, pelicans and Humboldt penguins. On our journey through Paracas National Park we saw flocks of pink flamingos standing next to the beach. It was the first time I had ever seen flamingos or penguins in their natural habitat.

Huacachina is a tiny town surrounded by gigantic sand dunes. Climbing to the top of them was like walking to the top of a mountain except much harder because our feet sank into the sand with every step. From the ridge where we watched the sun rise, sand dunes stretched in all directions for as far as we could see.

A popular sport in Huacachina is sand boarding which is similar to snow boarding but warmer. The first time we hired a sand board we had to turn back because the scorching sand was burning our feet. We tried it again close to sunset and had great fun whizzing down the slopes although none of us were able to stay on the board for long.

The highest sand dune in the world, Cerro Blanco, is in Peru. It is 2078 metres above sea level and measures 1176 metres from the base to the summit. We could see it from Nazca.

The famous Nazca Lines are huge drawings, made in the desert sand around two thousand years ago. They were created by taking away the darker stones from the surface to leave the lighter ground underneath. Many of the patterns are geometrical shapes or animal figures such as monkeys, fish, birds or spiders. Some of the designs are up to two hundred metres in width. It is not known exactly who made them or why. From the viewing platform we could just about make out the shapes of a tree and some hands but the best way to see the lines is from the sky in a plane.

We said farewell to the others at Nazca. Alicia and Alvaro were taking a different route but we hoped to meet up with them later at Machu Picchu. Harry and Ivana were planning to catch up with us in a few days time. We gave them each a friendship bracelet that we had bought from a stall near the

Nazca lines. Alicia and Alvaro gave me Bessie, their teddy bear so now there were four teddy bears on the tandem, Otter, Floppy, Patchit and Bessie.

A Spooky Story

Our spookiest experience happened on the day that we went to see the mummies at the mausoleum of Chauchilla. We had just left the town of Nazca and were heading out to the coast, when we spotted a signpost with 'Chauchilla Cemetery 7Km' written on it. Mum had been impressed by a postcard in the Nazca Lines museum showing a picture of mummies at Chauchilla and had wondered where it was so when she realised that it was on our route, she was keen to go and have a look.

We could see that the track would be very difficult to cycle on because of the depth of the sand which had accumulated on the gravel surface but it didn't take us long to flag down a taxi. Dad stayed with the bikes while Juan drove me and Mum down the dusty track.

The mummies of the Nazca people are about two thousand years old. The people mummified their dead by wrapping the bodies in embroidered cotton and painting the material with resin. They placed their dead in family graves, sitting down and facing east.

When we arrived, there was nobody else there (apart from all the dead bodies of course!) and it felt quite creepy. We were glad that Juan had offered to be our guide. The mummies were all just sitting there out in the open, in shallow tombs with adobe brick walls. Their faces were mainly skulls with very long dark hair although because of the dry desert climate and the methods used to preserve the bodies we could also see the remains of skin and nails. They all wore clothes.

Unlike museums containing ancient artefacts back home, there were no barriers or panes of glass separating the exhibits

from us and no 'Do not touch' signs. Juan kept leaning into the tombs and picking things up to show to us including skulls and bones.

The Nazca people put food and belongings in with their dead. Over the years the graves have been looted by robbers but we could still see the remains of pottery bowls and pretty woven bags.

Because Sean had to stay with the bikes, he never got to see the tombs. Juan told us that he knew where there were plenty of other mummies and offered to take us to see them. He drove us to his house and showed us into his back yard which was basically the desert. There were literally HUNDREDS of skeletons and parts of skeletons, half buried and littered across the sand, everywhere we looked!

'These are my ancestors!' he told us with a proud grin. He was clearly very much at home with his ancestors as every so often he picked up pieces of them and began to rearrange them, casually piecing together body parts to make a complete human!

'Here's a baby!' he said cheerfully, passing me a tiny, shrivelled corpse, still covered in skin. He tried to persuade us to take a few bones away with us but fortunately Dad politely refused although Juan insisted that we at least take away some small pieces of woven cloth.

Mum still thinks we must have been crazy not to carry mobile phones with us on this journey. I often wonder how we would have found each other again if we had got split up. Mum was the only one of us to even have an e mail address! When it came to hooking back up with Harry and Ivana we had to resort to the old fashion methods of leaving signs for them on the roadside.

Since we lost our Bob trailer flags in Honduras, we made another flag from a piece of yellow cloth that we found. It showed two adults and a child holding hands and had the words 'La Familia' written on it. It was something to do with the election but we didn't know what, hopefully nothing too controversial.

That night when we were camping in a quarry away from the road, we attached our flag to a tree at the entrance, along with an arrow and scratched a message onto a rock in the hope that our friends would see it.

I had found the whole Chauchilla experience quite unnerving and wasn't relishing the prospect of spending the night in a quarry in the back of beyond so I was delighted when, just before nightfall we heard the sound of laughter and cheerful voices calling our names.

For the next few days the road hugged the coast and our route was either on top of the cliffs or next to the beach where line after line of big white crested Pacific breakers rolled in. We had to battle against some very strong head winds and frequently the wind blown sand was piled up right across the road. Often in the mornings there was a heavy fog and everything was drenched in dew. We got soaking wet and chilled even though there was no rain.

The Inca Warning!

It was a long climb to Arequipa where we left our bikes behind for a few days and took the bus to Cusco, the capital city of the Incas, a mighty empire of twelve million people whose rule spread 2500 miles long and 500 miles wide over the Andes in the sixteenth century.

They were a very advanced civilisation for their time. In addition to building thousands of miles of very good roads, the Incas were skilled stone masons who could make enormous pieces of rock fit together like a jigsaw. In Cusco there is an original Inca wall with a famous twelve sided stone. There was a man in front of it dressed in the costume of an Inca warrior posing for photographs with the tourists.

Women and children, dressed in the local traditional costume, holding lambs and wearing tasselled hats which resembled lampshades also stood in front of the cathedral where people could photograph them for a small fee though when we visited the village markets we could see that this type of clothing is the everyday dress for many people.

We met up with Alicia and Alvaro and took the train to see Machu Picchu, the most famous of all the Inca ruins. First we went up a deep gorge surrounded by spiky mountains and snowy peaks until we came to the village of Aguas Calientes which means 'hot waters'. Mum and I went for a bathe in the public hot springs there at night when it was lit up.

When we went into town to buy our tickets there was a sign in the window which said this:

WARNING!

Sir Visitor. Welcome to Machu Picchu!
Please before approaching the bus it has his ticket from enter Machupicchu city inka since during a brief season podra to acquire it in center cultural of the inc. One of the town of hot waters to the flank of the church, in the following schedule.

Of 5am to 21.45pm

The ticket sale of entrance for Machu Picchu Inka is realised in permanent form in the city of Cusco in the Office of San Bernando

Note. As of Date the sale of tickets from enter Machu Picchu city Inka is NOT realised in the same city Inka

THE ADMINISTRATION

Mum said that it was probably because the writer had used a Spanish/English dictionary to translate the text literally word for word into English. No doubt, judging by the baffled expressions on peoples' faces, this is what our attempts at speaking Spanish came out like, when we didn't know the correct phrase and had to try and build our own sentences using a dictionary.

Next morning we got up at 4.30 and got on a bus which took us up a winding road through the jungle where we were surrounded by huge green cliffs. The first place we visited was the guardhouse which is where we saw the famous postcard view of the city with Wayna Picchu Mountain shrouded in mist. We were lucky to have got such a clear view. It was September and the rainy season was beginning. The previous six days it had been so wet that there was no view at all.

Once we had taken photographs of me, Alicia and Alvaro, my teddies, our family and two llamas mating in front of the famous view, we continued through the main city gate to the Temple of Three Windows. We climbed to the top of a tall tower called an Intihuatana which was used by the Incas to communicate with the sun god. At the top we saw a carved rock which astronomers used to plan the best times for planting their crops on the steps of flat green land which they carved into the slope. We also saw fountains and aqueducts for carrying water as the Incas were fond of bathing.

It would have been nice to have joined the A Team (Harry, Ivana, Alicia and Alvaro) as they cycled South through Bolivia passing the Salar de Uyuni, but we had heard that, in places, the roads were so terrible that cyclists have to pick up their bikes and carry them over the roughest parts. This would have been impossible with the tandem and trailers.

We really wanted to see the Basket Islands on Lake Titicaca so before we returned to Arequipa we took a bus to Puno. Lake Titicaca is the highest large inland lake in the world, on the Altiplano, the high plains of Peru and Bolivia.

We took a boat tour of the floating islands of the Uros tribe. The islands and houses are made from the totora reed which grows in the lake. The island which we landed on was about two metres thick and was floating in fifteen metres of water. It was over one hundred years old. They have to keep adding new reeds at the top because the reeds in the water slowly rot. We could feel the ground moving beneath us as we walked around.

The reed boats, which the Uros people row from one island to another, have amazing animal faces on the prow. As we were leaving, four of the ladies who had been selling souvenirs stood in a line and sang a song together, clapping their hands in time to the music. At first we thought that this must be some kind of ancient spiritual tribal chant of the Uros people. Gradually it dawned upon us that what we were hearing was in fact 'Baa Baa Black Sheep' followed by 'Twinkle Twinkle Little Star!'

CHAPTER 9

CHILE AND ARGENTINA

Homesick

Having become accustomed to an easier lifestyle in Peru, we had started to turn soft and Chile came as rather a shock. Everything was much more expensive so we could no longer afford to stay in hostels or to eat in restaurants. Once we crossed the border, we had to camp by the roadside once again and to buy all our food from supermarkets.

We had been a bit lazy with our Spanish, relying on our bilingual friends to do most of the communicating. This, combined with the fact that the Chilean dialect was far more difficult to understand than the more formal Peruvian Spanish, meant that we almost felt like complete beginners again.

After all the fun of being with the others, it felt quite lonely on our own. Up until this point I had really enjoyed the journey but now I started to long for my friends and to wonder what I was missing out on at home. I worried about whether Kaya and Élan would still be my best friends when I got back. Much as I loved my parents, I needed the company of people my own age.

It wasn't as if the scenery provided much distraction either. The road which we took went through the Atacama Desert.

This two thousand kilometre stretch of land is the driest place on earth. In some parts there has been no rain since records first began. There was nothing growing at all. For as far as we could see there was dust and gravel. It felt like we were cycling on the moon. In one small village where we spent the night, the owner of the guesthouse told us that he had lived there for the whole of his life and never once seen rain.

The towns in northern Chile were hundreds of kilometres apart so we had to pack food for seven days. We could only manage to carry twenty litres of water at once on the bikes, but luckily, about every hundred kilometres, we came to a Posada which was like a truck stop where we were able to fill up our water bottles. Without them it would have been impossible for us to have taken this route.

These sand blasted shacks, which reminded us of Wild West outposts, were like an oasis for us when we staggered in from outside, covered in sweat and dust, gasping for a large bottle of coke.

There is no water in the desert but we often saw what looked like big blue pools shimmering on the road and in the sand. They were mirages caused by waves of heat rising up from the ground.

Sometimes we had to dodge whirling dust storms which whip across the barren ground like mini twister tornadoes.

At least camping was easy. We could simply push our bikes off the road and pick a spot on the sand. Although there were no trees we still found plenty of wood from broken boxes which must have fallen from trucks so we had no problem making a fire in the evening. Because of the lack of humidity the stars in the night sky were amazing which is why so many of the world's space observatories have been built there.

Although we rarely got the chance to buy fresh produce, we occasionally found vegetables like onions and tomatoes which had been dropped on the road. One day Mum made a stew entirely from things we had picked up off the ground. She called it Pasta del Desierto.

We often got lost in South American cities because of the lack of road signs. In contrast on the open roads there seemed to be an abundance of them. Rows of gigantic warning signs were posted up to a mile in advance of the slightest bend or incline. Our hearts sank at the sight of a sign like this one:

Often, however, the slope which followed was barely noticeable. Our minds boggled when we came across a similar symbol to the one above, depicting a car driving over a completely horizontal piece of ground! Never underestimate a flat road surface!

This was our favourite sign of all, seen in Patagonia;

It means. 'Warning! Bad hair day!'

We passed by huge salt beds known as salars. Some salars are white and look like vast frozen lakes. Most of the ones that we saw in Chile were just huge expanses of brown cracked earth. The roads across the salars were completely flat and, when the wind was on our tail, our daily mileage exceeded a hundred kilometres.

We saw a large number of factories and mines in this area because the earth is rich in minerals such as nitrates, lithium, copper and iodine. Copiapo, where we spent a night, is close

to the San Jose gold and copper mine which had recently collapsed, trapping thirty three men for sixty nine days. Eventually a special rescue capsule was built so that they could be winched out safely. Happily all the miners survived.

Often places that were marked with a circle on our map, normally representing a town or village, turned out to be just the site of a factory or mine which was very disappointing when I had been looking forward to an ice cream for the last fifty miles.

Apart from a few ancient geoglyphs on the side of the road and El Mano del Desierto, a gigantic hand constructed from cement in the middle of nowhere, there wasn't much to look at so I read my Harry Potter book to pass the time.

Mum and Dad began to worry about me when I invented a game in which my right hand was one person and my left hand was another. My two imaginary friend hands had long, in depth conversations with each other while I was riding on the back of the bike.

When I had finished my schoolwork in the evenings I gave lessons to the teddy bears in maths, writing and geography. I felt that it was important for them to have a good education too.

After the town of La Serena the countryside became much greener. After days of nothing but brown dust trees and flowers were a welcome sight. There were farm stands by the side of the road where we could stock up with fresh produce such as olives, avocados, goats cheese, peaches, oranges, cherries, bread, honey and other foods, all locally produced and much cheaper than they were in the shops. Often when we bought something the stall holder would throw in a bag of fruit, free of charge.

There was also much more in the way of living creatures now. One morning Mum and I were lying next to one another in our sleeping bags with our knees up. Mum was reading me a story when, out of the corner of her eye, she saw some big dark hairy legs appearing over the edge of her knee horizon. She froze and told me to keep still while Dad fetched a cup and a map. Heading towards our faces was an enormous spider, about the size of my hand. Next

time we had internet access we googled it and found out that it might have been a South American recluse spider, another of the most poisonous spiders in the world. There were some gruesome images of the wounds on someone's hand a few days after being bitten, with gangrenous flesh hanging off exposed bones.

Another time we woke up to see an ant trail several lanes wide, marching from the head to the foot of the tent in between my camping mat and Mum's, entering and exiting the tent through small holes at either end. We had pitched our tent on their route and they had no intention of making a detour. It took all day to get all the ants out of our belongings.

One morning we were lying in the tent when the ground shook really hard for about ten seconds. It felt like we were on a train. There are a lot of earth tremors in this area. Earlier that year in February, Chile suffered an earthquake which measured 8 on the Richter scale. The tsunami which followed caused damage to many of the towns on the west coast, south of Santiago.

The Tandem gets Trampled and Broken

When we joined the motorway it became more difficult to find places to camp. Barbed wire fences stretched for miles along the side of the road, preventing access to the fields on the other side.

We were camping at a public picnic site one night when we had the most bizarre experience which nearly put an early end to our journey. A bus stopped and a group of very high spirited people jumped out and started to fool around next to the tent. We couldn't tell if they were drunk or crazy but they were bouncing around the bins and on the tables and trying to make us dance with them.

The way they were behaving was making us feel uncomfortable but we tried to be polite and friendly. However, before we could stop them, five large adults climbed onto the tandem and, before our eyes, the whole rig crumpled.

While we stood and gaped at our bike in horror, the whole

party ran away and climbed into the bus which sped away. Mum chased after it in vain, swearing and throwing stones.

Initially it appeared as if the whole bike was wrecked but, on closer inspection, it turned out to be just the wheel rims that were broken although the frame was always slightly misaligned after that. Mum and I had to stay at the rest area with the tent and all the gear while Dad hitched for twenty miles back to the last town where he could find a place to get the wheels fixed. It was a whole day and night before we saw him and an anxious time for us all – yet another time when a mobile phone would have been very handy.

When we were cycling along the motorway we looked forward to arriving at the Copec filling stations where we could buy a *completo*, a jumbo hot dog with a variety of sauces such as guacamole. Occasionally for a treat we went into a posada and bought *cazuela*, a bowlful of meat, potatoes and vegetables in a soupy stew.

I had my tenth birthday in Santiago. Mum and Dad splashed out on a posh hostel with a swimming pool which was lit up with different colours at night. My present was a portable DVD player and a pile of DVDs which Mum had bought for a dollar each at a Peruvian market. We could watch a whole film in the tent before the battery needed to be recharged.

South of Santiago we began to see snow capped volcanoes in the distance and soon we were glad to escape from the motorway and ride inland to the town of Pucon, on the shores of a large lake beneath Volcan Villarica.

At the time this was Chile's most active volcano and we could see a big plume of smoke billowing out from the crater at the top. Since then Villarica has erupted. The videos of the explosion in 2015 are spectacular. Over three thousand people were evacuated from their homes.

After Pucon we cycled over the Mamuil Malal pass into Argentina, our fourteenth country. The road was so steep and gravelly that we had to push our bikes for ten kilometres until we reached the top of the pass in Volcan Lanin National Park where there is another snow capped volcano and forests of araucaria trees. We can often see araucaria trees in Britain. We call them monkey puzzle trees and they have been introduced into gardens over here from places like this.

We made it to the town of Junin de los Andes just in time for Christmas day where we treated ourselves to a room for the first time since my birthday, three weeks ago. Dad and I made a Christmas tree out of a cardboard box and glitter. Mum helped me choreograph a nativity play for my teddy bears to perform with costumes and stage sets. Otter was Mary. Patchit was Joseph. Bessie, Floppy and Barbie were wise men and my Sylvanian families were the shepherds. Little Ducky, who we had found abandoned on the motorway, was baby Jesus.
We all sang Christmas carols (apart from Dad).

We bought a cooked chicken which we ate with instant mash and Mum got tipsy and a bit maudlin on Chilean red wine. When we crossed the border into Chile, Mum had been delighted to discover that, although food was more expensive, red wine cost less than two dollars for a litre and, because it was sold in cartons as well as bottles, it was easy to pack on the bike.

Plagues of Locusts and Hurricane Force Crosswinds

The Lake District in Argentina is very pretty with forests, mountains and crystal clear lakes to swim in. The road verges were filled with lupins and the houses look like Swiss chalets on the cover of a chocolate box. Everything is very expensive.

In Argentina everyone drinks mate tea which is made from coca leaves. They put the tea in a little round pot called a gourd and drink it through a hollow metal tube like straw. They carry it with them and pass it around to their friends.

The shops were full of jars and cartons of a sweet toffee sauce called *dulce de leche*. It is basically the same as condensed milk boiled up to make caramel, like the kind we use in millionaire shortbread or banoffee pie. Mum bought it to use as a spread to put on bread because it was cheaper than chocolate spread or peanut butter which cost about $12 for a jar in some shops. After a while I found it rather sickly.

After Esquel we left the mountains behind. For two days the road was covered with huge locusts. Some were flying. Most were on the ground. There was a dark bloodlike fluid all over the road where cars had crushed them and other crickets were feasting on the carcasses. When we stopped for lunch it was difficult to find a place which was clear of the carnage of huge dying insects and I found that it put me off my food.

The Patagonian Steppe is a vast flat empty plain also known as the Pampas. There are no trees – just tufts of brown spiky grass and thorny bushes. It is very bleak. The land is used mainly for farming sheep and cattle. Apart from the occasional estancia or ranch we saw no buildings for hundreds of miles.

Big ostrich like birds called rheas or *nandu* ran alongside our bikes followed by their gigantic baby chicks. Every now and then we saw an armadillo crossing the road. Herds of guanacos, wild llamas, were everywhere.

Ruta 40 was a tough place to cycle because there was no shade from the sun or shelter from the wind. The swarms of biting *tabanas* made life particularly unpleasant. Imagine the horse flies or clegs that we have in Scotland then times it by ten and that is what these insects are like. Even when it was windy they managed to find parts of our bodies that were on the sheltered side and they could bite through our clothes easily. The bite hurt as badly as a wasp sting and came up as huge red lumps which turned septic on our skin. Give me our Scottish midges any day!

The winds which were usually blowing from the side, increased in strength until it was impossible for us to stay on our bikes. One day we had to walk and push for fifty kilometres. We lost count of the times Mum fell off her bike, once in front of a passing bus and onto a cattle grid. It was frustrating and scary and there was more than the average amount of shouting,

swearing and tears amongst the Tomlinson family on that road.

To make things worse, one of the self inflating camping mats kept going flat. It must have been a fault with the valve because no amount of patching would help it stay up. It was unlikely that we would find anywhere to buy a new one now so, to make it fair, we took it in turns to sleep on it. By the end of the journey two of our mats had deflated permanently so we all took turns to use the good mat, meaning that, one night in three, each one of us got a comfortable night's sleep.

Last week Mum was sorting through our camping gear when she thought she had found an extra mat. When she opened it up, she saw, written along the top in biro, in her own handwriting, 'THE FLAT MAT, Dad's latest excuse for being an arse in the mornings!' The joyful memories of our harmonious family times together all came flooding back.

While we were waiting (in vain) for the winds to die down we stayed at the small town of Rio Mayo where the one big event of the year, La Festival Nacional de la Esquila, a sheep shearing festival, was being held. Experts from all over Argentina compete to be the fastest and most skilled at shearing a sheep.

By the looks of things the sheep being sheared were the lucky ones. *Asado* is a barbecue of sheep or lamb and can often be seen at public events in Argentina but to us the bodies of several sheep split in half and roasted on iron crosses over the flames of a huge fire, watched by spectators in cowboy costumes, was a grizzly sight.

We stopped at the touristy village of El Chalten for nearly a month because we wanted to go hiking in the Fitzroy mountains in Los Glaciares National Park. They are very spectacular with huge rocky spires and jagged peaks on top of an enormous ice field called Campo de Hielo Sur.

The problem is that the mountains are very nearly always hidden behind the clouds. We waited for two weeks to get a glimpse of Cerro Torre but when the sky finally cleared the view was so impressive that it was well worth the wait especially early in the morning when the first light turned the snow crusted mountains a glowing pink.

On the campsite we met cyclists of many different nationalities because El Chalten is at the southern end of a famous cycle trail called the Carretera Austral. We made friends with Yoko and Hiru from Japan, who were cycling around the world. Yoko, whose name means 'child of the sun' taught me how to write my name in Japanese. Pippa and Liam from London invited me to stay in their chalet for a sleepover to give me a break from Mum and Dad. We also met a French couple on very strange looking bikes called recumbents. They looked as though they were almost lying back on an easy chair with their feet up in front of them.

We hiked up to Laguna de los Tres to see Cerro Fitzroy and up to Laguna Torre for a view of Cerro Torre, a 2000 metre high needle of rock, plastered with ice. Although it is only 3128 metres high, the summit was not conquered until 1974, much later on than the first ascent of Everest. This is because it is so difficult and dangerous. The weather is nearly always stormy with freezing winds of 100 miles per hour at the top of the pinnacle which can only be reached after forty hours of continuous vertical climbing. Once thought of as impossible, it has only been scaled by a small number of elite mountaineers and has kept its reputation as one of the world's most challenging peaks.

At El Calafate we took a bus tour to see the Perito Moreno glacier. Considered by many to be the 8th wonder of the world it is over sixty metres high and six kilometres wide. The glacier is advancing and sometimes moves forward as much as two metres a day. About every four or five years the glacier reaches the shores of Lago Argentino and a portion of the lake becomes dammed against the huge wall of ice, causing the water to rise to sixty metres above the surface of the main part of the lake. Eventually the pressure builds up so much that the ice wall ruptures and causes a spectacular calving as the blocked up water bursts through, sending an explosion of ice into the lake, a spectacular show for the people who are lucky enough to be standing on the viewing platform on a day when it happens.

This was not one of those days. We stood in the pouring rain for two hours until a piece of ice the size of a football plopped gently into the water. Eventually we decided to sit in the visitor centre and watch video footage of the glacier calving in the sunshine while we waited for our bus to arrive.

The campsite in El Calafate had a common room with a television and as I watched it I realised that it was Valentine's Day. My unromantic parents hadn't remembered so I made a card for my Mum. It said 'To the best Mum I've ever had on Valentine's Day. PS Dad sends his love (maybe)' Mum laughed so much that she choked on her sandwich.

It is against the law to take food into Chile, even from Argentina. This law is enforced very strictly as we found out later on our bus journey back to Santiago when we were all held up at the border for hours because an orange was found in a passenger's handbag. We camped on the roadside just before the border and ate every remaining piece of food in our barrels.

We were relieved that the small village of Cerro Castillo had a small shop where we were able to stock up on meals for the two hundred kilometres of dirt road which we were about to take through Torres del Paine National Park, yet another world famous landmark and the scenic route to Puerto Natales. It is also much more challenging than the alternative way on the paved Ruta 9. We had been warned by other cyclists that it was very steep, bumpy and rough.

Our hearts always sank whenever we saw a signpost with the word RIPIO written on it. It means gravel road and usually, for us, meant that we were in for a rough ride.

We were glad we had resisted the temptation to stay on the tarmac as the weather was clear and sunny, giving us great views of Los Torres, (The Towers) and Los Cuernos, (The Horns). The lakes were bright turquoise like the ones in the Rocky Mountains. One day it was so hot that we went for a swim but the water was ice cold so we only stayed in for a second.

The Cold Completo

When we finally arrived at Punta Arenas it felt very strange. After two years on the road we had reached the end of our journey. It was a bit of an anticlimax as there was nobody there to meet us or celebrate with us.

We stopped at a garage and bought hotdogs but the hotdogs were cold.

At the hostel there we met up with a lovely couple of cyclists called Ali and Ana. They treated us to a big dinner in a restaurant which cheered us up considerably.

We were sad to say goodbye to our trusty tandem but we needed money for transport back home and Dad got talking to two guys at the hostel who were looking for bikes to cycle the Carretera Austral northwards. It was nice to know that it was going to be taken on another adventure. We heard from them after they had finished their trip and were glad to hear that the owner of the bike shop in Bariloche bought the tandem from them because he wanted to go travelling with his son. We often wonder where it is today.

For an end of trip treat we took a boat to Magdalena Island in the Strait of Magellan. Between November and March sixty thousand couples of Magallenic penguins come here to breed and give birth to their chicks.

The boat journey took two hours. The island is tiny with a lighthouse in the middle. As we approached we began to see hundreds of little black and white dots all over the rock which turned out to be penguins. Visitors to the islands are told to stay behind the tape to give the birds their space but we saw plenty of them standing next to the path and even on it and they seemed to be very tame. Many of them were in the process of molting and were an adorable combination of feathers and fluff.

Before we flew home from Santiago we took the bus back to San Martin de los Andes for the wedding of Harry and Ivana, a beautiful ceremony high in the mountains. I got to wear a pretty dress instead of smelly cycling gear and the teddy bears, who were guests of honour, dressed up in smart suits. We gave them Mum's bike as a wedding present. They have visited us in Scotland and now have two little boys. I hope that one day we will all go on another big cycling adventure together.

That was five years ago. I'm a teenager now at Plockton High School and life is so busy with school work, friends and social events that it's difficult for me to leave home for very long without missing something important.

Mum usually insists that we still at least do one interesting thing each summer for fear that we might start 'stagnating'. I cycled my own bike from Land's End to John O Groats last year and we often paddle our sea kayaks along the Scottish coastline so the house continues to smell of 'Trip' from time to time, but it's been a while since we've had a really big adventure.

Otter, Floppy, Patchit and Bessie seem to be a little restless these days. They have developed a tendency to go exploring on their own at night, mainly underneath the bed. Otter still mysteriously disappears from time to time and turns up again a day or two later in odd and unexpected parts of the house.

Perhaps the teddy bears are trying to tell us something!